THE ONLINE JOB SEARCH SURVIVAL GUIDE

Everything You Need to Know to
Use Social Networking to Land a Job Now

Paul Borgese

Sherrie A. Madia, Ph.D.

Full Court Press

Full Court Press
A Division of Base Camp Communications, LLC
3 Woodstone Drive
Voorhees, NJ 08043

Find Us Online:
OnlineJobSearchBook.com

Library of Congress Cataloging-in-Publication Data
Borgese, Paul, and Madia, Sherrie Ann.
The Online Job Search Survival Guide by Sherrie Madia and Paul Borgese.

Summary: Best practices for implementing sustainable social media strategies for job search success.
  p. cm.

ISBN: 978-0-9826185-3-0

2010929363

Printed in the United States of America

10 9 8 7 6 5 4 3 2 1 First Edition

CONTENTS

FOREWORD

RECENTLY, I WAS CATCHING UP WITH my business school mentor, Douglas "Tim" Hall, a professor of Organizational Behavior at Boston University and a true guru when it comes to the topic of career management.

Given that I've spent 15 years helping college students conduct professional job searches, Tim and I were discussing the role of higher education in preparing young professionals for the workplace. Tim noted that there are many great universities that do an excellent job of finding initial placements for their impending graduates…but are they really doing a good job of preparing young professionals for the ongoing, lifelong process of career management? When it comes time for their *second* jobs after graduation, will they have any idea of what to do beyond contacting their alma maters in hopes of help from the alumni networks?

This is troubling, especially in the face of a 21st-century job market that is unprecedented in its complexity. The Sunday newspaper classified sections have all but disappeared. Myriad Internet sites have stolen their niche, and the job seeker of today must have some degree of technological savvy to compete.

The good news—and the bad news—is that online job listings and applications have made it easier than ever for job seekers to become aware of employment options and to go after them. Although it's initially comforting to see that there are numerous sites with dozens of seemingly plausible jobs, the trouble is that thousands of other job candidates can see and apply for them too. So in the midst of a difficult economic time in the United States, what are candidates to do in order to ensure that their resumes get pulled out of the massive pile and put in front of a manager who might hire them?

As Paul Borgese and Sherrie Madia show in this book, job seekers can no longer ignore the power of social media networks in the hiring process. Increasingly, such sites as LinkedIn are critical in building an interpersonal network that absolutely can open doors to job opportunities at an individual's "target" employers.

Rooted in the same concepts that marketing experts use in positioning products and services for a targeted segment of consumers, Borgese and Madia show job seekers how to build social networks online and ultimately leverage them as they prepare themselves for job transitions, either sooner or later. They also highlight many other keys of the job-search process, including the targeting of employers, fundamentals of interviewing, and numerous online resources.

For me, though, the most powerful message of the book is that social media networking is by no means an instant gratification scheme. You can't "friend" someone in Facebook today and expect him or her to help you find a job tomorrow. You may make a LinkedIn connection this week that leads to a job opportunity in two years. The building and maintenance of relationships takes time and vigilant effort to produce results. The most important takeaway is that we *all* should think of our current employment situations as temporary. So what are we doing to get ready for the next move? If we have shown due diligence in creating and nurturing an online presence characterized by positive communication and helpfulness toward others, we are bound to benefit in turn eventually.

In these days of economic uncertainty, offshoring, downsizing, and corporate acquisitions, you never know when you'll need to find your next position. Think of your investment in social media as analogous to going to the gym regularly. You may not always feel like doing it, but do it anyway, and do it consistently. When it comes to social media, this book will whip you into shape, but it will be up to you to make sure that your online network is in peak condition when you need to muscle your way past other job seekers.

Scott Weighart
May 2010

Scott Weighart is the author of several books on career development, including *Find Your First Professional Job and Exceeding Expectations: Mastering The Seven Keys To Professional Success*. He has over 15 years experience in consulting, higher education, training, and recruiting. For more on his books, visit www.mosaiceyepublishing.com.

ACKNOWLEDGMENTS

AS WITH ANY PROJECT OF THIS NATURE, the work is always a team effort. And *The Online Job Search Survival Guide* team was truly first rate. We would like to thank those who helped with their valuable assistance, including Lisa Burke, Caitlin Drummond, Sherry Hoffman, Charles Kim, Robert Moskowitz, Kathy Shaidle, and countless colleagues from across industries and disciplines who offered their generous insights. We would also like to thank Scott Weighart for his thoughtful introductory remarks. If you are new to job search using social media techniques, we offer our thanks to you for your willingness to try some new approaches to finding your next job and to shaping your lifelong career—and of course, we invite you to share your success stories. Let us know what worked for you so that we can share your experiences with others. Write to us at contact@onlinejobsearchbook.com.

PREFACE

WHAT MANY JOB SEEKERS ARE REALIZING—
often the hard way—is that the traditional approach
to finding a job is no longer viable. In fact, some would
argue that the online approach has become the mainstream means
of finding gainful employment. If you've been out of the job-seekers
market for a while, you may be surprised at how much has changed.
The days of scouring the Sunday newspaper for help-wanted ads
and then mailing off your resume are long gone. If you're entering
the professional workforce for the first time, you need to understand the ground rules in order to make the most of your time and
energy when it comes to securing a job.

Between the current economic conditions and the ongoing
online evolution, the marketplace has gotten smaller, while the
means of promoting one's personal brand have increased. Therefore,
job seekers must approach their searches in an unfamiliar way:
Establishing and promoting their own personal brands.

The old approach to job seeking went something like this. The
job candidate would:

- Develop a resume
- Locate potential jobs by scanning online and offline job
  postings
- Write a cover letter, then submit the resume and cover
  letter to job banks and organizational sites

- Begin the waiting game, hoping for a call from the employer

In order to compete in today's job marketplace, applicants must change their approaches to how they're going to secure their next jobs—and then how they're going to keep them. They also must keep their networks active should something unforeseen occur. To ensure that your employment search begins with the best chance of success, you'll need more than just an updated resume. You will need a well-crafted and finely tuned message. Thus, the first section of this book focuses on the concept of *positioning*.

Today's unemployment rate remains dismal, and the U.S. continues to see stagnation in new job creation. Couple this with what will be approximately 1.5 million newly minted college graduates at the time of this writing—almost all seeking jobs—and a decrease of approximately 13% in jobs posted online, and the picture doesn't look bright. And yet, a beacon of opportunity amid this gloomy landscape awaits candidates who are willing to put in the time to differentiate themselves from the rest of the pack.

Thus, *The Online Job Search Survival Guide* is about turbo-charging your job search by leveraging the powerful reach of social networks. The book offers proven and effective online job-hunting strategies along with tactical steps designed to help you to find your next job faster and with targeted efficiency. If you're a job seeker, you have no time to waste. *The Online Job Search Survival Guide* takes you through a clear, step-by-step process that will jumpstart your job search immediately and optimize your ability to secure the ideal job. This process of positioning includes:

- Strategies for online research, job searches, and personal brand building

- How to rev up your efforts to land a job NOW from your "Web 2.0 resume" to your online presence, to showcasing yourself as the ideal candidate for any employer in any market. To do so, we show you how to use everything from search-engine strategies to LinkedIn, Facebook, Twitter, social networks, blogs, podcasts, video, and more to leapfrog the competition and to land yourself a job.
- Core tactics for selling your product—you!—in all that you do, from your personal brand to your letter of inquiry to acing a job interview

The Online Job Search Survival Guide is a surefire way to significantly—and rapidly—improve your odds through actionable social networking tactics along with online job search do's and don'ts for landing—and keeping—your next job as well as positioning yourself not just for a job but for a lifetime personal brand designed to keep you in demand in the marketplace. Beyond simply explaining how to conduct a 21st-century job search, we help you understand the context of the brave new professional world. In Part II of this book, we describe how this is essential to the step of targeting. The insights in this section include:

- The changing job market landscape and the concept of multiplying your contacts by connecting to other people through a "people search"
- Effective job/people search preparation, including job/people search strategies and tactics
- The importance of social networks and social media
- Incorporating social media and social networking into your job search

The third section of this book focuses on *landing* a job as well as on what you will need to do *after* you obtain your job to position yourself for future success with your personal brand over the course of your career. To this end, we provide stories from real people facing real economic challenges who landed real jobs using social networks. We share their success stories in the hope that they will inspire you to do more than just read this book and shelve it afterward. View this book as an important guide in your quest for a job. It is designed as a tool not just to be read but to be applied right away. If you activate the tactics in this book, you will find a job. But remember, like anything else, social networks work only if you're willing to work at them. This isn't about an effortless search: It's about a smarter, more targeted, and strategic approach to job seeking.

Some elements of what you are about to read reflect more traditional forms of networking. Other aspects reflect the overhaul of networking that has come about due to the Internet. We discuss how any successful professional today needs to blend traditional approaches with cutting-edge social media tactics in order to maximize the effectiveness of any job search.

If you can master these concepts, old and new, you will be ready to maximize your ability to obtain the job of your dreams.

PART I

Positioning

1

Social Networks and the Successful Job/People Search

Fundamentals of Social Media and Social Networks

FOR STARTERS, let's briefly reflect on what we mean by **social media** and **social networks**. **Social networks** refer to online communities of people who share common interests. Members of a social network use these communication platforms to set up personal profiles, which include information about themselves. They then can search for, contact, communicate with, or otherwise share information with others in that community. Examples of popular social networks include Facebook, LinkedIn, and MySpace. Although social networks were created for personal relationships, job seekers should think of social networks as distribution platforms that enable them to broadcast their messages to others.

The term **social media** has been used interchangeably with social networks. However, social media is a bit more broad-based in that it includes channels of distribution (e.g., blogs or Web-pages) beyond the social networks (communities). The most important element you must consider is that social networks and social media are all about *content*. And when it comes to your job search, the content you create for each channel must position you in a way that your target audience (e.g., the industry, company, human resources recruiter) will find most appealing. Social media enables you to distribute information to large numbers of people (for example, making your personal information available for viewing by the public). How you shape the content that you will post or upload as a blog post, an article, a video, or a podcast will have a major impact on the type of employers you will attract. Self-publishing their qualifications, skills, accomplishments, and personality gives job seekers more opportunity than ever before to promote themselves...*and more risk* unless they have a full understanding of all that the online job search entails.

The Best Approach: A Blend of Traditional and Social Media Elements

The most successful job searches are neither dumb luck nor magic. They are developed from strong networks that the job seeker has already built, both online and off. Effective job seekers must integrate social media outreach with the more traditional approach in order to present a consistent, aligned, professional image. Recruiters are evaluated in part based on their abilities to screen qualified applicants, so they don't react well to surprises, such a candidate whose interview presents an entirely different person from what is stated or implied on the resume. Job seekers often forget that human resource professionals are looking for the candidate they saw on paper, online, and in a profile photo—so consistency counts!

The best recommendation is that job seekers include links to their blogs, LinkedIn profiles, YouTube video resumes—whatever online elements they have created—on their traditional resumes. Standardize profiles across all social media sites, and link them together.

Candidates must position themselves effectively where recruiters are searching as well as become content producers in order to attract recruiters directly to them. Again, bear in mind the current state of the job market:

- Fewer jobs are available.
- More competition exists for those jobs.
- More touch points exist for job seekers and recruiters to interact.
- Smart job seekers must optimize their personal brands and seek out those who are on the lookout for great candidates.

In addition to the standard-issue background and employer checks, hiring managers—and even college admissions officers—are turning to social networking sites to delve more deeply into the backgrounds of applicants. If you think this is unfair, think again. The Internet is not a private club for you and your friends. It's a public space. The rule used to be that anything on your resume was fair game for an interviewer to consider. Although this is still the case, the same is now true for anything on the Internet that has your name attached to it—including your Facebook wall. If you don't like the odds that a recruiter will check out your wall of potentially inappropriate updates, our best advice is to clean your wall.

Like anything else in the realm of social media, we do not advocate that any candidate forego traditional job-search fare in favor of a strict social-media diet of job search. Candidates should continue to post their credentials to job banks, respond to corporate postings, attend career and job fairs, and so forth. That said, note that this type of activity would have been primary in the past, but today's candidate needs to have a 21st-century mentality about job search. Although some attention should be devoted to traditional job search methods, the majority should be geared toward social media strategies—regardless of industry or job type. Social media is simply a more efficient way to find yourself a job sooner rather than later.

Social Networks and the Successful Job/People Search

Social networking gives job seekers the distinct advantage of having one more type of weapon in their arsenals of tactics. When confronted with an unexpected layoff or a corporate downsizing, job seekers usually react in one of two ways:

- They take immediate action, sending a barrage of resumes through the digital space without even mulling whether to update that resume.
- They slip into sweatpants, fall into a funk for a while, and consider writing that novel they've started on and off for the past 11 years.

We'd like to encourage a different reaction altogether: a strategic and reasoned approach to not only securing a job but securing *the* job that best suits your skills and your passions. In the mix of all this, however, is our innate tendency to be slow to act when it comes to networking. Quite frankly, most people would sooner not go out and network face to face if they could. They would much rather network from the comfort of a La-Z-Boy™ recliner with laptop in hand.

Yet what this book will show is that job seekers must be willing to get out of their comfort zones to test many different ways of connecting with people during their job searches. While it is never easy to be out of a job, today's applicants have an unprecedented advantage by having primed social networks available and at their fingertips in ways that simply weren't available to job seekers even a handful of years ago.

No One Is Exempt from Job Seeking

Okay, if you're one of the few who are independently wealthy, then perhaps you needn't worry about a job. But the vast majority of us are not exempt. You may be highly educated, highly skilled, highly motivated, or all the above. You might be just starting out fresh from high school, trade school, or college. Regardless, job-seeking savvy will give you a critical advantage.

Perhaps you have changed jobs frequently. Have you ever been called a job hopper? Maybe you've been downsized or flat-out fired from a job or two. Some of you have gone through the humbling experience of having to trudge to the unemployment office for a canned orientation and an interview with an employment counselor. Regardless of the reasons behind your job search, the experience always comes with an ample dose of pain, frustration, and anxiety.

Let's face it. Being out of work, feeling unsure about your future, and having to look for a job is likely one of the more memorable times in your adult life. And we don't mean the good kind of "memorable"!

But the forecast for your job search is only partly cloudy. This book offers practical and tactical ways to help you get the jobs you want as quickly and as painlessly as possible. Obtaining a great job may not happen easily or immediately, but the goal is to move in a positive direction as opposed to being like a gerbil on a wheel—moving frantically but getting nowhere fast.

Remember that being out of a job is not the end of the world. For some, it may represent a crisis, but it's also an opportunity. A job search offers individuals time to reflect and to consider new directions. Our advice is to view unemployment as an opportunity to reposition, to reestablish, and to rethink an important part of your life. After all, it's never "just a job"—it's 80 percent of your waking life—so you might as well make it count! What type of work would be most meaningful and rewarding to you? With patience, persistence, and a tactical approach, you will give yourself every opportunity to land your dream job.

JOB SEEKER SUCCESS STORY:
The Architect of Job-Seeking Success

Brian Ward, a resident of Cleveland, Ohio, knew he had to act fast to find work after losing his job in 2008. Ward beat the normal 12-week job-searching grind by capitalizing on shrewd use of the Internet. Remarkably, he landed a job in just 11 days.

Ward is a married architect with three children. He is the sole breadwinner for his family. Like so many Americans, though, he found himself unemployed when the economy turned sour.

While he had "passively" been updating profiles on Facebook as well as on the Twitter and LinkedIn social-networking sites, Ward started making phone calls within the first three hours of joining the ranks of the unemployed.

One of those calls was to a college friend in North Carolina who used Twitter extensively. The friend sent out messages to all his contacts, giving Ward the idea to use the medium as a way to enhance his search.

Ward spent his first jobless weekend updating his existing profiles and uploading a new resume to the professional networking site LinkedIn, and he sent messages to his 200 Facebook contacts about his job search.

Within a few hours of starting his search, Ward was able to line up a phone interview with a Louisiana company that employed one of his friends. Although that interview did not result in a position, the quick turnaround did strike Ward as "impressive."

In addition to posting on the sites and joining groups to get his name and qualifications out into cyberspace, Ward also attended a webinar presented by a former arena football player to get tips on looking for work.

Ward proceeded to spend 12 to 15 hours each day in his quest for employment. He updated his Facebook and Twitter accounts, and he sent frequent emails to provide his contacts with information about his search and to thank those who had been assisting him.

Finally, a former co-worker set up Ward with a contact at her firm. He got the job. The co-worker sent him a half-joking message, asking why Ward did not appeal to her about openings at the company. It had never occurred to Ward that a former subordinate may have been in a position to help him in his search.

"It's still all about connections," Ward said. "What's changed is how you do it."

SOURCE: Kiviat, Barbara. "Using Twitter and Facebook to Find a Job." *Time,* 8 June 2009 <http://www.time.com/time/business/article/0,8599,1903083,00.html>.

Have a Roadmap

How will you get where you want to go without a roadmap? If you're like most people, you might be inclined to job search on instinct or to let the marketplace of available jobs dictate how your search will go. Today's job seeker cannot afford to take this loose approach.

Frankly, the majority of job seekers don't have time to wander aimlessly through the process. They have mortgages to pay, families to feed, and expenses that won't wait. So rather than find yourself hopelessly stranded on a dead-end path, we arm you with directions—and a few shortcuts—on the road to your next job. Of course, you'll also need a steady dose of motivation to keep going when the job seeking gets tough.

Your job search may be urgent, or you may have the luxury of more time to plan. You might be just starting your career, or you might be in the midst of a career change after many years or decades. Regardless, our strategies and tactics are equally applicable. All successful projects start with the end result in mind, and your job search is no exception. Making your goal as clear and specific as possible is critical.

Think Temporary

Over a lifetime of employment, always remember to maintain this mentality:

Every job is temporary.

By no means are we suggesting that you should be disloyal to your employer or that you should work as if you have one foot out the door. However, you should always approach any job with an eye toward what's next. This philosophy will keep you in a professional development mindset and thus allow you to take advantage of every opportunity to advance your skills from any position.

You must be willing to acknowledge and to accept the reality that it is highly unlikely that you will stay in one job for the duration of your professional career. Those days are largely gone.

Of course, you need to commit yourself to doing the best job possible. Great performance always opens doors eventually. But by accepting and realizing that all jobs are temporary, you will position yourself to remain alert and to optimize your efforts toward obtaining a recommendation or referral when you need one. In essence, you want to find yourself in a constant state of readiness to look for another job at a moment's notice.

Taking this stance can help you avoid being caught off guard with no safety net or Plan B should your employment situation change unexpectedly. It also will make you less likely to knee-jerk and to immediately write off opportunities that may arise over the years. As the saying goes, "The best time to look for a new job is when you already have one." Just because you're relatively happy in your present job doesn't mean that there might not be something better out there. From a practical standpoint, it's wise never to become too trusting or overly comfortable in what may become your "temporary" position. Always have a Plan B that you can activate quickly.

Be sure you have two items in top shape and ready to go at all times—your attitude and your resume.

Develop Your Strategy and Tactics

When you are first launching your job-search campaign, we suggest that you take a page out of the military playbook by thinking through your strategy and related tactics. We cannot overstate that almost all successful projects are well planned. Sure, there are stories about how someone's best friend got a job by slow dancing with an HR recruiter at a wedding, but these are flukes and not sustainable strategies in the long term.

Most people will spend more hours of their lives in their places of employment than at home with their loved ones, so you really want to think through your job and career.

Don't wing it. Make sure you have a strategy BEFORE you start sending out resumes.

Your Strategy

In the field of marketing, strategy consists of two components: targeting and positioning. When it comes to marketing yourself, *targeting* is the process of deciding which fields you want to consider and which organizations you want to approach for a job. *Positioning* refers to how you want to present yourself in order to maximize the opportunities of being hired by your target organizations.

Your Tactics

Tactics are the actions, activities, and tasks that you must perform in order to achieve your strategic objectives. In this case, that means finding the job that you want. Here are some examples of tactics you may employ:

- Writing articles about your areas of expertise
- Posting blog entries
- Creating personal profiles on social networks
- Researching job boards to help you position yourself correctly

Likewise, here are some strategic questions you must consider before beginning your job search:

Targeting:
- What job types, companies, or industries are you planning to target?
- What sources will you use to research other target organizations that might meet your job-hunting criteria?
- Which social networks will help you connect to people who can then help you contact key people in your target set of employers?

Positioning:
- What are the most effective ways of presenting yourself to your target organizations? What is your marketing message or, as it is sometimes known, your 30-second commercial or 60-second elevator pitch?
- How does your message to individuals in your social networks differ from the message that you present to prospective employers? That is, how do you present yourself to those who may recommend you to others who could ultimately give you a job?
- What information will you include in your profile pages when you post them on social networks?

- Is your message targeted enough? Will you create different versions of your pitch to meet the needs of different companies that you target?
- How will you go about actually connecting to people on social networks?
- How will you use blogging to help you market yourself? Will you become a blogger yourself or maybe comment on other peoples' blogs?
- Will you create a video of your 30-second commercial or 60-second elevator pitch?
- What will you do to monitor and to manage your online reputation?

Knowing the answers to questions like these before you start looking for a position will help save you time, money, and energy during your job search.

Take the time to think through your strategies and tactics at the start of your job search, and you'll save yourself a great deal of frustration along the way.

Although it's a trite expression, remember that clichés often stick around because of their simple truth: Remember that those who fail don't actually plan to fail—they simply fail to plan.

Getting Fired, Downsized, or Whatever You'd Like to Call It

When you're out of work, you are very much focused on yourself. This is only natural.

As such, you may find little consolation in knowing that there are many others who are in the same situation as you. There are also most likely some who are even worse off than you are. Unfortunately, in the last several years, several million hard-working folks have lost their jobs.

The recent job-loss hit parade has been particularly horrendous, hitting every industry sector and negatively affecting the lives of millions of individuals and families.

In light of the catastrophic economic collapses we've seen during the nation's worst recession since the Great Depression, candidates must be smarter than ever in the face of fewer jobs and sky-high unemployment.

Regardless of the causes, we are all in a new world in which job seekers must be brave and ready to approach job seeking in a truly unique way. Social media can provide you with the tools you will need to showcase yourself—or to reinvent yourself—so that you may thrive amid any market conditions.

Why the New Hypercompetitive Job Market?

We don't need to tell you how competitive today's job market is. You know that companies around the world are competing against one another to offer quality products and services at the lowest possible costs. Companies are sending jobs overseas if they can cut costs by doing so. Alternatively, they are simply shedding jobs by the thousands in order to stay profitable.

In many places, there are far fewer locally based businesses that are thriving or even surviving. Many have either been acquired by out-of-town owners or have been put out of business by large multinational corporations with daunting economies of scale, such as Walmart.

Unfortunately, many of these larger corporations don't share the same sense of responsibility, loyalty, and commitment to their employees and the local communities in which they do business—unlike their former owners. Regardless of what the corporate mission statements say, many employers don't value their employees as individuals as they once did.

In the past, company CEOs and presidents may have known all their employees—and even their employees' family members—on a personal basis. Now it's every employee for him- or herself. Often, the pace of business is too fast—and job turnover is too high—for anyone to really get to know anyone else. This is the reality that you must face as a job seeker.

Generations ago, you were considered a job hopper if you didn't stay at a company for at least 10 years. In today's workforce, getting a new job every two to three years is more of the rule than the exception.

As sad as it may seem, all employees are replaceable, and, eventually, most employees will find themselves replaced in one way or another—if not by technology, then by a younger, faster, more tech-savvy generation with skill sets that have naturally evolved to fit current job markets.

The days when companies valued and rewarded employee loyalty above all else are largely gone. Many employers have gravitated to an extreme fixation on bottom-line results. If you don't produce, you're gone. If you are uncertain as to where a company places its values, it's best to operate under this assumption.

In fact, many executives at today's largest companies view their employees as disposable commodities, regardless of the impact that has on employee morale. If you have not yet experienced such a climate within your professional career, don't assume that it doesn't exist: Assume you've just been lucky.

So maintain a realistic mindset about your relationship to your employer. They owe you pay and benefits, and you owe them a solid day's work. There are no guarantees beyond that. Even though many would love to return to that golden era of secure employment, there is no turning back.

Accordingly, do yourself two big favors:

- Accept the realities of how these and other factors have negatively and irreversibly altered the global employment landscape.
- Always keep the positioning of you foremost in mind. Each job seeker must fend for him- or herself. However, through social networks, fending for yourself can occur within a community, thus lessening the feeling that you are going it alone.

Job Market "Ins" and "Outs"

Just as global economics have had a profound effect on how companies deal with their employees, cultural changes and technology had a profound effect on how you should go about searching for a job. If you have been out of the job market for a while—or if you are just entering the ranks of the employed and reflecting on the way in which your older brother obtained his first job years ago—remember that the Internet has been driving dramatic change in recent years. Specifically:

- Paper resumes are out. Online resumes have been in for some time now. But most recently, those who employ social media tactics have had a significant advantage over those who aren't familiar with such online techniques.

- Classified ads in newspapers are out. Online job boards, such as Monster.com and HotJobs.com, are in. But even more cutting-edge are social-networking sites.
- Meeting face to face for first interviews is increasingly being replaced by initial telephone interviews. Most employers are unwilling to waste the time, money, and effort to organize and to meet face to face with job candidates before they have weeded out those who don't meet their criteria via phone calls, videoconferencing, and Web chats. So you need to get your message down. It has to make an impact quickly, or you're dead in the water.
- There is an increasing move away from centralized cube workplaces. Employers are finding that they can cut costs and achieve higher productivity if they have at least some of their employees working remotely from home.
- Having human resources executives shuffling through paper resumes is out. Automating the job candidate screening process by using job sites and scanning software to home in on qualified candidates by finding keywords in their digital resumes is in.

Unless you have been completely cut off from civilization, you are fully aware of the economic employment mess we face, not only from a U.S. perspective but from a global standpoint. Therefore, an effective and successful job search today requires flexibility in adapting to the changes that have occurred in the employment market.

Whether you are comfortable with the idea or not, you must acquire and use all the job search skills, knowledge, and marketing vehicles available.

The bottom line is that if you are not using all the tools available, especially social networking and social media, you're putting yourself at a major competitive disadvantage when job hunting.

Reach Out and Touch Someone

Remember the phone company commercial from years ago that used the jingle of "reach out and touch someone"?

Well, that is precisely what you have to do in your job search—reach out and connect to people.

But now, with social networking, you can do that much more effectively online. Online social networking can save you the time and frustration of having to get dressed up and go out to random networking events where you may or may not meet people who can help you find a job.

As anyone who has tried that tactic knows, real-world networking events give you plenty of opportunity to meet people who are looking for a job—just like you. Unless your goal is to commiserate with peers, that doesn't help you much.

Before you get too comfortable in your sweatpants and slippers, you will still need to show up at face-to-face networking events. In addition to this, though, you must now spend part of your networking time online. This will not only help you meet people; it will help you meet the *right* people *faster*.

The Internet: Both Good and Bad News for Job Hunters

The Internet has brought us true global connectivity.

It is a game-changing channel that has forever altered how you and everyone you know—and don't yet know—relate and interrelate with one another.

From one perspective, this is great news when it comes to expanding the number and type of jobs that you might be able to find. Additionally, the Internet also can help you find that next job faster.

Over the past decade or so, such online job boards as Monster, Yahoo! HotJobs, Dice, CareerBuilder, Careers.com, and others have come into their own and made significant inroads in the traditional way of applying for jobs.

In part, that's been driven by ever-increasing numbers of job candidates online. Simultaneously, employers have increasingly shifted their talent acquisition efforts to the Web. By tapping into social networks, you'll greatly improve the odds of finding your next job more efficiently.

2

The Brand Called "You"

Building Your Brand Message

I N 1997, *FAST COMPANY* magazine ran a cover story by Tom Peters entitled "The Brand Called You"[1]—and caused a sensation. Overnight, a new phrase entered the business lexicon: "personal branding."

Tapping into the zeitgeist with impeccable timing, Peters made the following clear: If you're wearing other people's brands from head to toe, why not become a brand *yourself*, so you'll stand out in a competitive world?

Nowadays, nobody works at the same firm for 40 years before retiring with a handshake and a gold watch. These days, Peters observed, we are all "free agents in an economy of free agents"—the "CEO of Me, Inc."

---

[1] Peters, Tom. "The Brand Called You." *Fast Company* 31 August 1997
< http://www.fastcompany.com/magazine/10/brandyou.html>.

"Ask yourself the same question the brand managers at Nike, Coke, Pepsi, or the Body Shop ask themselves," Peters counseled, "but this time, pretend that *you* are the brand."

"What is it that my product or service does that makes it different? Give yourself the traditional 15-words-or-less contest challenge. Take the time to write down your answer. And then take the time to read it. Several times.

"If your answer wouldn't light up the eyes of a prospective client or command a vote of confidence from a satisfied past client, or—worst of all—if it doesn't grab *you*, then you've got a big problem. It's time to give some serious thought and even more serious effort to imagining and developing yourself as a brand."

Detractors complained that "personal branding" was just a flaky fad, a slick new synonym for age-old concepts like "image" and "reputation." Others warned that Peters's advice reduced human beings to mere commodities or encouraged navel-gazing narcissism.

So much for the naysayers: Over a decade later, that personal branding "fad" has become a career-counseling cornerstone.

We know that attraction-based marketing results in job offers to applicants. In a tight job market, it's more important than ever for candidates to consider their personal brands. The personal brand, generally showcased through candidate-generated content, is a nonintrusive means of putting yourself in front of recruiters in a strategic way.

So just what is personal branding?

First, here's what personal branding is not:

- It isn't a title or job description or a laundry list of degrees, awards, and accomplishments.
- It's not about nonstop, gimmicky self-promotion.

- And it definitely isn't about wearing a "signature" perfume or "trademark" power tie. Those tangible affectations are things, and a brand isn't just a thing—it's an idea.

A famous brand is much more than its familiar trademark. Think about it: Nike sells style and image, not just shoes—and certainly not "swooshes." Successful branding instantly evokes tangible and intangible associations that prompt consumers to choose that product over all others.

It also inspires confidence. As one expert put it, good branding conveys "a promise that must be delivered."[2]

Personal branding is no different. The fact is that everyone *already has* a personal brand. The bad news? Not everyone realizes it yet.

"If you aren't actively creating your own brand," warns culture watcher David Chen, "other people and companies will do it for you. Whether it's what Google says about you when people search for your name or what your co-workers say about you when you're not listening, the brand called you will be created; it's just a matter of whether or not you want to be involved in the process."[3]

Personal-brand creation doesn't have to be complicated. In fact, it is preferable to have a simpler-is-better mentality, as long as the result isn't generic, corny, or flippant. Personal branding also doesn't have to be slick and sleazy, either.

Think of it as an elevator speech but about a *person* instead of a *project*. Take an honest personal inventory. Brainstorm by asking such questions as:

---

[2] Hansen, Randall S. "Building Your Career Brand: Five Tools for Job-Seekers."
< http://www.quintcareers.com/career_branding_tools.html>

[3] Chen, David. "The Brand Called You: Ten Years Later." *Buzz Marketing* 28 August 2007
<http://www.pronetadvertising.com/articles/the-brand-called-you-10-years-later34500.html>.

- What is my proudest professional accomplishment?
- What am I famous for?
- Am I the "go to" person when it comes to one field or subject? If so, how or why?
- How do I add real, measurable value?
- How do I make other people's lives better and easier?

Brand strategist Catherine Kaputa tells job seekers to "find the 'white space'—a brand position that *you* can own, that's not associated with anyone else. When communicating your uniqueness to others, use analogies, such as, 'I'm a cross between X and Y,' or 'I'm X on steroids.'"[4]

JOB SEEKER SUCCESS STORY:
Post Actively, Post Often

Barbara Maldonado used the LinkedIn professional networking site to quickly snag a new marketing job for a suburban Chicago firm.

Maldonado, 32, was already part of a marketing group on the social networking site and had made several contacts there. When she was laid off from her former job, it was one of those contacts who told her about an opening at his company. The contact liked how she responded to a question in the Innovated Marketing, PR, Sales, Word of Mouth & Buzz Innovations group and stayed in contact with her.

When she posted news about being laid off on the site—which now has an estimated 40 million users—her contact let her know about the position she now has. "Without actively participating in that discussion, I would not have made the contact for that job," Maldonado said.

---

[4] Kaputa, Catherine. "How to create a winning impression with an elevator speech." Execunet Newsletter. 11 May 2010. http://catherinekaputa.com/?cat=7

Maldonado is one of many professionals using social networking to their advantage. The various sites are becoming popular among corporate recruiters and others making hiring decisions. The networks are also embracing the more professional side of profiles. Facebook, Twitter, and others are beginning to recognize the business applications for members as well. Facebook has recently started posting business profile pages in addition to those of individuals.

Sandra Fathi, a social media expert and president of Affect Strategies, says these sites are a great way for people to stand out among other candidates for open positions: "Not only are employers looking for better candidates, but ones versed in social media and seeking out opportunities." Employers are also using the sites, in some cases, instead of job boards or traditional classified advertising to seek out candidates.

SOURCE: Dickler, Jessica. "I Found My Job On Twitter." CNN/Money.com, 12 May 2009 <http://money.cnn.com/2009/05/12/news/economy/social_networking_jobs/index.htm >.

Here's a memorable tip from *Me 2.0* author Dan Schawbel:

"I typically recommend your personal brand statement to be about five words, that states your expertise and who you serve. For example: 'I'm the best brain surgeon in Boston.'"

"Think unique positioning," adds career coach Susan Britton Whitcomb. "Be a 'St'. (pronounced 'Saint'), as in the beST, firST, or moST. Are you the *best* at creating product marketing strategies, are you the *first* one to have mastered how to conduct electronic meetings for your work team, and are you the *most* accomplished, award-winning sales professional in your company/industry?"

Avoid hype. Be authentic.

Once developed, a personal branding statement should be incorporated into resumes, cover letters, and e-mail signature lines as well as throughout social media. Although it doesn't have to be constantly repeated word for word—in fact, it shouldn't be—

that personal branding statement should nevertheless inform and inspire one's online persona.

Visibility is important, but be professional, too. Leave consistent, recognizable digital footprints on Twitter, Facebook, LinkedIn, ZoomInfo and other online properties that reflect a polished image.

As noted earlier, hiring managers and recruiters use social networking sites to source and to investigate candidates. A forgotten blog, a Twitter account with only a couple of posts, or a LinkedIn profile that isn't 100 percent complete will leave a poor impression.

A professional homepage and online resume/portfolio—complete with a "first name, last name" .com domain name—is the perfect place to display a personal brand.

Job seekers whose vanity URLs are already taken can try adding a middle name, "Ph.D.," or a similar distinguishing word. Then reserve that as a username across various social networking sites using NameChk.com; the days of getting away with "Andy12345" are over.

William Arruda, personal branding expert, suggests going beyond the traditional resume and using a "brag sheet" that speaks to your top five strengths and how you have used each one of those in a specific situation with a measurable result.

Because personal branding is about standing out from the crowd, creating a video resume or a mock video "interview" might be a smart decision, too. Such sites as like CareerBuilder and Vault are now offering video-resume hosting. Keep it brief, professional, and not gimmicky. But be warned—unlike a traditional resume, a video resume can go viral, damaging one's personal brand:

"Last fall a Yale graduate sent his video to a major Wall Street investment firm," writes recruiter Joe Turner, "and later found his video posted on YouTube, mocked throughout the Internet for its preposterous, bragging style."

Good personal branding radiates success. People like to work with competent, accomplished, even powerful individuals. But as that painful example above demonstrates, overt self-promotion is a career killer. So is narcissism and selfishness.

Ironically, personal branding might more accurately be described as "interpersonal branding." Nurture your network to take advantage of word of mouth; focus on what you *uniquely* can offer others. Leaving a tidbit of practical advice on a comment thread makes a much better impression than a self-aggrandizing "personal statement" squeezed into an excessively long "look at me!" post.

Likewise, employers don't care about a job seeker's "objectives." They want to know what you can do for *them*. Why not use that valuable resume real estate for a personal branding statement instead, one that focuses on what you will bring to the organization, not what you want to get out of it?

Personal branding is an ongoing project. So is the reputation management that goes along with it. Because most Web searchers never look past the first page of Google results, job seekers need to "own" those top 10 results for their names.

That's why taking control of your identity on Facebook and other popular sites is so important—it's a way to "push down" negative references to the relative obscurity of page two or three of Google or other search engines. Such companies as PeoplePond and QAlias can also help manage this sort of "personal SEO."

Other firms, such as Defend My Name and ReputationDefender, help "eliminate digital dirt," says Arruda, by trying to remove unflattering personal comments and online "smear campaigns" altogether.

So what's the payoff? Branding consultant Chuck Pettis tells the story of a client he helped "brand." The client was a middle manager who went into her annual job review with a new outlook and attitude. Her supervisor asked her the usual question about what she hoped to accomplish in her position during the coming year.

"Previously I simply said, 'I'd like to do more training.' Now I have real ammunition that lets me say: 'There is a recognized need in the library for more training, and these specific managers want me to do it. Furthermore, I'd like to put my analysis skills to use by assuming a leadership role in the implementation of a new library management system.'"

Now imagine being able to bring that kind of specificity and self-awareness to a job interview. A potential employer will have a hard time forgetting a job candidate like that. Such is the power of personal branding.

3

Your Social Media Resume

THE CONCEPT OF THE SOCIAL MEDIA RESUME developed in the first half of 2008—some reports say it was Christopher Penn who came up with the name and idea.

Not a resume in the sense of a traditional paper document, the social media resume includes your resume, PLUS the sum total of "you" online, specifically geared to your work life and experience.

This can include your various social networking profile pages, audio podcasts, video clips, articles you've written, forum posts you've made…to name just a few possibilities. It can cover anything about your unique skills, personality, background, expertise, and achievements—all revolving around your employment background.

The social media resume can be a source of angst for job seekers—particularly those who had a hard enough time with putting together a conventional resume. But the social media resume is worth the extra time. Once you have a solid traditional resume in place, the social media resume becomes an exercise in showcasing your strengths as well as your skills in the online space.

The value of the social media resume is that job seekers are able to create substantive and accessible resumes for hiring managers that reflect their personals brand and their positioning in relation to the candidates' desired employment opportunities.

In essence, social media has enabled job seekers to reverse-engineer the recruiting process. Instead of submitting their resumes *out* to employers, their resumes become vehicles to pull employers *in*. They are basically walking billboards of qualifications and credentials that can be searched and shared.

The easiest way to begin is to create a Web page or blog. There are many free openware applications that will enable you to establish a presence on the web For example, WordPress and Typepad are two very user-friendly solutions. If you decide you'd like to get a little fancier, most free applications also have paid versions, which can enable you to do a bit more. For most job seekers, freeware works just fine.

You will need to purchase your domain name, as this will be key. Sample URLs that work well include yournameresume.com, yourname.com, yourname.net, or yourname.org. Once you have the domain name and your page has been set up, you'll want to include this URL on everything: business cards, paper resume, sample work, or other marketing materials you might create as part of your job search.

In order to create a stronger presence, multimedia comes next—provided you are comfortable in this space. If you freeze up in front of a camera or find an audio recording fails to represent your true strengths, you'll have two choices: Practice until you get it down pat, or skip this step. If you are able to add multimedia, you will create a unique and saleable advantage.

There are many options: Adding a very brief video or audio segment in which you give your 30-second pitch on why an employer should hire you is a good idea. You can shape targeted statements that capture the responses to basic interview questions. These serve as audio and video testimonials to your character and professionalism—and to the authenticity of your responses. To this end, you must be certain that the statements you create capture the essence of the responses you would provide during a face-to-face interview. After all, companies will be looking for consistency. The content you create should then be included on sites that enable sharing, as well as included on your Web page or blog.

Job seeker Amanda Casgar[1] created a video resume in an effort to land a social media job at the Murphy-Goode Winery. Casgar was responding to the California-based winery's job posting for what they termed a "lifestyle correspondent." It was a job that entails what many companies are seeking in candidates: the ability to create personal connections with their consumers. Because Casgar was vying for a social media job, specifically, she began tweeting about wine, creating a Web site called "Goode Times with Amanda Casgar." She started a Facebook fan page and created a video resume. Although the job she was applying for made her skills in social media as important as the content itself, this approach can work effectively for all candidates, regardless of job type.

The benefit of an effective video resume is that few people actually have these, so your video segment will serve as a differentiator in the recruiting process (at least for now).

The best video resumes have several key attributes:

- They are short (no more than three to four minutes).
- They describe the value you will bring to the position you are seeking.

[1] Holson, Laura M. "Tweeting Your Way to a Job." *New York Times* 20 May 2009 <http://www.nytimes.com/2009/05/21/fashion/21whiz.html?_r=3>.

- They tell why you are the best candidate for your desired job.
- They offer a few insights into your character, ideally in a narrative, conversational style.

If you tend to turn into a "deer in the headlights" whenever a camera is pointed in your general direction, then video is not for you. Don't simply create a video to say you have one. Use this only if you are comfortable with this medium, and don't post your final video clip until you get it right.

In addition to posting your video to YouTube, you will also want to add links to this content to your social network profiles, such as Facebook or LinkedIn, but be sure to update or clean them up first. The last thing you want to do is create a reason for an employer to become disenchanted with you based on a foolish photo or a raunchy comment on your Facebook wall.

The social media resume has the added benefit of showcasing your ability to navigate the social media space. Increasingly, this is a plus across jobs and across industries. A simple share tool widget is typically available as a part of most basic blogware and Web site tools, and including such sharing features will enable visitors to increase your presence by posting your credentials. This will help get your resume seen by more than just recruiters, so you will want to take advantage of this.

Some job seekers are hesitant to share their resumes in the social media space. But much of the concern may be unfounded. Top professionals have their bios posted all throughout the online space. They include contact information and have established presences. Aren't you hoping to get your resume seen by more hiring managers rather than recruiters by adding to social networks? Remember: Visibility creates opportunities.

Depending on what statistics you cite, some form of referral or networking plays a part in anywhere from 60 percent to 80 percent of job vacancies that are filled. Keep in mind that many great job opportunities are only available through the "hidden job market" and are never posted to the public, it's easy to see that you're missing out on a large part of the job opportunity pool unless you are "plugged in" and using social networking when in the market for a new job.

This is even more important when competition is extraordinarily intense, as it is today with less jobs all around.

Will a Social Media Resume Work for Anyone?

As we described earlier, a social media resume can be an extremely valuable tool because it *pulls* employers to you instead of forcing you to *push* your resume to them. That said, there are some caveats to bear in mind before you go this route.

A social media resume is best for a candidate who has a very clear and relatively narrow "brand." If your education and experience scream out that you are a great market researcher (or business analyst or recruiter), and you are looking strictly at opportunities that represent a logical progression in your field, then a social media resume is a terrific tool.

But what if you are a candidate with a relatively broad range of skills and experiences who is perhaps pursuing two or three different job niches? Here's an example: Let's say that Susan has been a fifth-grade teacher in a private school. She reaches a stage where she wants to move on to another job. But what sort of job? She's thinking that she *might* want to stay in a classroom teacher role, but she's weighing the trade-offs between an inner-city public school classroom versus simply moving to a different private school catering to relatively wealthy families. Yet a part of her would like to get out of the classroom altogether and try her hand at a job in the corporate sector—most likely in training and development—or maybe even an academic advising role at a university.

This is all entirely plausible for Susan, yet it presents problems for her if she wants to create a social media resume. For some job seekers, the concept of *versioning* is very important. While we delve into this more in Chapter 4, it's worth describing briefly here.

What Susan probably needs to do is think of numerous versions of how she presents herself. She may need as many as four different resumes to reflect her varied interests. All her job experiences will be the same, of course, but how she slants or "spins" each job may vary depending on whom she's targeting with her resume. As such, a social media resume may not work well for her.

With social media, the name of the game is authenticity. Thus, versioning is totally appropriate with individual resumes and individual searches. In contrast, a social media resume is intended for a broad audience, and thus the content must be more inclusive and present a consistent picture of the candidate.

In other words, a social media resume might actually do a disservice to Susan. If she attempted to put one together, she might end up coming across as a wishy-washy candidate with all too many irons in the fire. Even worse, she could come across as an insincere individual due to the incongruity between her broad version of herself online versus any attempts she would make to come across as focused on a narrow niche in an interview for a specific position.

So for the majority of individuals, a social media resume can be a great asset. However, it can be a liability for those who need to position themselves in different ways for different jobs.

JOB SEEKER SUCCESS STORY:
A New Job before the Old Desk Is Packed Up

Jen Harris only took a few minutes to find a new job thanks to the Twitter social-networking site.

When Harris found out she was going to be laid off from Idaho-based MPC Computers, she immediately sent out a simple status update: "just been laid off from MPC."

By the time she had finished packing up her desk and prepared to leave the parking lot, she had a job offer from a friend who owned a local Web development company.

Twitter allows users to send out 140-character status updates in real time. The succinct form of these updates mirror longer ones popular on such sites as Facebook and MySpace that can include text, pictures, and videos.

Although Harris's search was unusually brief, getting the word out to peers following you on such sites as Twitter can greatly help and hasten the effort of marketing yourself within a professional community.

Professionals in the recruiting field recommend using these sites by joining groups or network communities in your given field of expertise. They also caution that impressions are very important, and applicants should monitor their profiles on the more social sites, such as Facebook, for any inappropriate material. More and more employers are becoming adept at social-networking, and an estimated 79 percent say they check a job candidate's social site before deciding to hire him or her.

If you are not in any of these groups, you can look for blogs related to your profession and post to them to show your expertise in a given field.

SOURCE: Dickler, Jessica. "I Found My Job on Twitter." CNN/Money.com, 12 May 2009 <http://money.cnn.com/2009/05/12/news/economy/social_networking_jobs/index.htm >.

Mainstreaming

If you're not using social networking and social media to help you with your people-search efforts, you're just sitting on the side of a river, watching job opportunities rushing by.

Using only or mostly more traditional job-seeking efforts and posting to online job boards is akin to sitting on that riverbank and tossing your fishing line in, hoping for a bite from employers.

You need to start *mainstreaming* yourself immediately and jump into that river of opportunity. A social media resume is the vehicle that can help you drive you into that river and surround yourself with far more exposure and job-opportunity potential.

Turning the Tables

Another benefit of using a social media resume is that it completely shifts the job-recruiting dynamics in your favor.

How? Simple.

Traditional methods of seeking employment use a "one-to-one" approach or a combination of "one-to-one" and "one-to-many" approaches. In other words, you find one job opening and send out one resume, or you do that in combination with posting a resume on a job board.

However, the "one-to-every" approach of a social media resume allows the universe of potential employers looking for your unique talents to be able to find you versus you working so much harder to find them.

This approach effectively "turns the tables" on the traditional recruiting process, and it turns them in your favor. In the "old" way, you'd "push" your resume out to limited opportunities you'd identified. With this new "one-to-every" approach, you change your limited "push" to a very strong "pull" mentality. Instead of you going to employers, your social media resume broadcast "pulls" interested parties to you.

That universe includes recruiters seeking candidates on behalf of their clients, companies searching directly online, entrepreneurs looking for risk-taking employees to join an exciting start-up. Basically, it includes anyone.

There is an added bonus. By including information in your social media resume about the type of opportunity, company, and culture you're ideally seeking, you can help "filter in" career opportunities that are a much better fit for you.

Your Online Footprint

It's all about expanding your online "footprint" or exposure.

Having *no* online footprint equates to only reaching employers that you contact. Having a *small* online footprint equates to reaching a smaller number of employers who know about and can find you.

To use an analogy, there's a place in England called Poets' Corner dating back several hundred years. Here, poets took turns reading their creations to a captive audience. Anyone who wished to speak about any topic could deliver his or her message to whoever wished to listen. Now just imagine doing the same thing, but on a global scale and to a massive audience.

That's exactly the difference between using a social media resume and more traditional job-search methods.

The social media resume helps create a global audience and reach out to many more folks who would likely have an interest in your skills. Just like the historic soapbox that allowed speakers to personally connect with their audiences, your social media resume does the same thing today. You allow potential employers and recruiters to "personally connect" with you and to actually "see" your personality and communication skills in action by incorporating video or audio clips.

In essence, your social media resume can help you develop a large online footprint and transmit your message more effectively. A massive online footprint equates to reaching far more employers, many of whom you'd never find out about on your own. They now have the opportunity to find you, and thus you have increased your potential job opportunities. The size of your online footprint does matter when it comes to seeking employment.

Your Personal Storefront—Where to Hang Your Shingle

You'll need someplace from which to "broadcast" your online presence and social media resume.

If you already have a blog, adding your social media resume creates a powerful platform for making others aware of your skills.

If you don't have your own blog yet or your own personal URL, either of these is a good place to start, depending on what sort of time commitment you are willing to make toward expanding your socia-networking efforts.

To be most effective, a blog should to be regularly updated and kept "fresh" at least once per week, but preferably daily or at least numerous times per week. This doesn't mean hours of work—just a brief period of time for an update.

That might mean a couple of paragraphs of fresh content around your area of expertise—perhaps some views on your industry, commentary around new products, a fresh opinion on some business aspect, and so forth.

Adding something of value to the community in which you would like to be gainfully employed can be a tremendous advantage when it comes to your job search.

Register "YOU"

If you haven't yet done so, it is highly recommended that you register your name in the form of your own URL (http://www.donjuan.com, http://www.princessleia.com) and with the ".com" extension ideally.

This is a great way to help create/extend your online footprint and to build your own personal brand. What's more of a unique, individual brand than "http://www.yourname.com"?

Registration is easy and inexpensive at one of many domain name registrars (a fancy name for a place to "register" your own name/URL). GoDaddy.com is a very popular and cost-effective option. As of this writing, one domain name will cost approximately $10 per year.

Simply visit one of these domain registration sites, and do a lookup for "yourname.com" in the search box tool to make sure no one else with the same name already "owns" it. If it is available, consider one of several related suggestions the registrar company might offer that would still contain your name.com in the URL.

If that isn't possible, or the suggestion isn't grabbing you, try "your-name.com" (hyphenated version).

If you have the option of getting yourname.com and the hyphenated version, take them both. You can always redirect or point one to the other. This way there's no potential confusion between two different people with the same name having almost identical

URLs—and having an employer going to the other person's site and not finding you there!

Search engines, such as Google and Yahoo!, are more likely to list such a Web site when people do a search on your name, because they assume that sites with such addresses are highly relevant to the person doing the search. So grab it right away!

It's very important to remember that you need to reregister one year later and for every year after that. Otherwise someone with the same name can grab "your" URL out from underneath you, leaving you with a bit of a problem in finding/choosing a new URL name.

Design Considerations

Graphic artists, web designers, interior designers, clothes designers, and landscapers all deal with design concepts, colors, and layouts, so those professionals have it relatively easy. Professionals who are less astute in these areas may have the best of intentions when it comes to resume design…but their efforts don't always come off well.

As you only have one chance to make a first impression—and with a social media resume, you're trying to impress MANY people—it's crucial you follow key design/layout principles to ensure you DO. So let's take a closer look at some essentials in this area.

Social Media Resume Aesthetics

1. Make It Easy to Read
- Use a sans serif typeface/font in a 10- or 12-point font. It's far easier to scan through than a serif typeface.
- Use a solid, lighter color background (no deep purple background with white type, no bright green or screaming orange backgrounds).
- Use black type color—this copies best if your resume is printed and passed around.
- Use a color wheel to help you look at and choose the most readable, easy-on-the-eye color combination.
- Keep graphics small and to a minimum. No distracting background images or wallpaper.
- Avoid animation, unless you're in a unique field (e.g., video game programmer) where this would be an asset as opposed to a distraction. Even then, less is more. You can always show off your portfolio/creations in separate attached links or files for those who want to see more of your work.
- Make it easy to "navigate" and find different "parts" of your social media resume. Try to use the three-click rule: If people have to use more than three clicks to get from the main page to where they want to go, that's too many (too frustrating and time consuming). Make it EASY and FAST for the viewer to get around.

2. Use a Clean, Simple Layout
- Don't get too fancy or complex.
- Use "bullets" like this, textual bolding, italicizing, and section headings appropriately. Make it easy on the eyes and easy to follow.
- Remember the "KISS" formula ("Keep it simple, stupid").

3. Use Consistent Formatting
- Keep your font style the same throughout for easy reading/scanning.
- Use selective bolding, italicizing, and underlining where appropriate and with the same areas (e.g., like these section headings—bold and italicized to set them off or to introduce a new thought).

A clean, simple design, layout, and formatted social media resume—just like with your paper resume—are far more preferred by recruiters and HR staffers than something really fancy. Remember, they're concerned with finding the right skills for a certain job. They could not care less about the coolest Flash-enabled animation you put together, and it makes their jobs harder if they have to battle with a program that may be incompatible with their systems. That's NOT how you want to impress.

Becoming Multidimensional

Unlike a one-dimensional paper resume, your social media resume allows you to communicate and to convey much more of who you really are. You are a multidimensional talent that cannot be captured on a page or two of paper.

Paper resumes have done the job up to now and will continue to fill a need for folks to physically "hold" something when reviewing the credentials of or interviewing job candidates.

But, let's face it: Paper resumes are generally dull—black color on white, sometimes cream-colored paper. Employers can't hear or see you…and getting a "feel" for you is at best a roll of the dice.

One of the benefits of the social media resume is that you have a blank canvas on which to paint a Technicolor portrait of yourself—complete with live audio and video if you choose.

You can show an incredible variety of your best traits in action. Here are just a few examples:

- Presentation excerpts
- Audio clips of your advertising
- Video clips of client testimonials or professional referrals
- A short pitch about how you deliver optimal customer service
- A speech at an industry seminar or trade show

These options will show off much more than your skills. They give you an opportunity to showcase your personality and character. All you'll need to do is apply your creativity and imagination. And you'll need to decide how much of yourself you choose to reveal, including elements from outside your work life. But sharing *some* of that judiciously can help employers connect with you.

The takeaway here is to remain focused on your main objective—and to keep everything professional.

Include Your Social Network Profiles

Whether you're just getting started or are on multiple social networks, you'll want to include those page addresses on your social media resume. Facebook, LinkedIn, and a host of other social network sites will allow you to create and then to embed a "badge" on your social media resume.

Although it may go without saying, we've seen too many candidates—and employees—fall victim to situations in which their social network pages introduced elements to employers and influencers that they later wished they had not revealed. In particular, we have seen individuals post photos of themselves clearly very intoxicated and only partially dressed, from wild parties. Likewise, some people post statements on Facebook walls that include sexual content or other questionable material.

Failure to secure text or photos of a more personal nature behind security features offered by social network sites can end up costing you interviews and potential job opportunities.

Of course, the best advice is to avoid posting these items in the first place.

Keep one simple rule in mind when it comes to social media: If you've posted content to a public site—regardless of the privacy settings you have put into place—then it's public content. This means that friends can share and forward it, and items meant for only a few eyes or ears can quickly turn viral—and not in a good way.

The upside, however, is that including your current social network profile pages on your social media resume helps show those interested in you the types and numbers of contacts you have and potentially deal with...as well as your involvement with the online global community.

Motivate with Multimedia

Incorporating some multimedia in or on your social media resume allows you to further customize your online brand and presence, but don't overdo it.

Well-chosen photos, video clips, audio MP3s, client and character testimonials or references, a quick elevator pitch on your core skills, podcasts, and other media are all great ways to bring your otherwise one-dimensional resume to life with a social media resume.

For example, instead of traditionally listing your achievements as on a paper resume, you could have a link to a short video of you talking about them. This gives you more time to expand on exactly how you made them happen, and you can also showcase your oral communication skills simultaneously. That's the great double-dip benefit of using multimedia rather than a paper resume.

Another great way to strengthen your case is to use a strong professional or character audio reference. You can ask your reference to focus on a carefully crafted list of talking points rather than replying to an HR staffer's randomly asked questions that may or may not bring out specific key expertise. YOU can completely manage the image you want and need to convey, thus enhancing your odds.

Overall, strategic use of multimedia elements in your social media resume can create an emotional connection with potential employers. Employers *want* to like you, and multimedia is one way to build rapport. After all, employers tend to hire candidates when they perceive that they a share connections with them.

One final thought on this topic: If your communication and/or presentation skills need polishing, take as much time as necessary to refine them through rehearsal. This will ensure that you project yourself as positively as possible. You only get one shot at impressing an employer, and you can do yourself a great deal of harm if you fail to make a good impression.

Lastly, be yourself, and be natural. No one wants to hire someone who sounds like they're reading off a set of cue cards or a prepared script. Practice, practice, and practice some more until you're completely relaxed giving your presentation.

It will pay off in spades, as employers increasingly value strong communication skills.

Keywords and Optimization Are King

Researching and placing select keywords are vital in ensuring that your paper resume rises to the surface. Social media resumes are no different. Here again, it's about creating exposure for you and your background.

Part of this depends on how you structure your social media resume. You might make it a stand-alone single page like your traditional resume, or you could break it into specific sections (skills, certifications, references, achievements, markets worked in, products sold).

Breaking it into different sections can allow you to target and to optimize specific keywords around related content for each page. Conceptually, this is very similar to optimizing individual Web sites and pages in order to drive traffic and to rank high in search engines.

What does optimizing do? When done properly, this type of targeting can help these separate pages rank higher on search engines when someone searches for you and specific keywords. This can help more employers and recruiters find you, resulting in more potential job opportunities. Try using two to three related keywords per page and its related topic.

Thus, if you have a single-page social media resume, you'll be limited to using just two or three keywords. Also, they'll likely have to be of a more general, broad nature. This can make optimization—and thus visits from interested parties—more challenging.

Make Your Social Media Resume Easy to Share

You have little to no control over which specific people visit your social media resume. However, if they're looking for your skills and have potential interest in hiring you—even if they are only influencers in the hiring process—you want to make it easy for them to spread the good word about you by sending your resume along.

That's right: It's about further improving your odds. Doing all the little extras can add up to a bigger competitive advantage for you:

- Set up reciprocal links to and from various social media vehicles and tools.
- Put a small form on your social media resume that allows people to e-mail/forward your resume to interested parties.
- Get the URL of your social media resume listed on as many networking sites as you can manage. Interest in your skills and experience can come from anywhere. Sometimes leads come from downright obscure and implausible places. Don't knock anything until you give it a try.

Don't Ignore the Stats

The cool thing with Web pages—and having your own URL is one of those—means you can capture all sorts of neat information in the form of statistics you can use to your benefit in your search activities.

You can then use this info to help refine your online marketing activities. Are the right people looking for you and finding you? Are the keywords you are optimizing having the desired impact? Are your tactics helping improve your online visibility? The stats will give you plenty of insight here.

The fancy name for this is "Web site/page analytics." Basically, this means using a simple statistical package that often comes with Web-hosting services to allow you to find out the answers to the aforementioned questions along with other interesting tidbits of information:

- Number of visitors who come to your social media resume
- Which pages your social media resume links to and which pages are linking back to it
- Keywords used to find your social media resume

Web analytics is a far deeper and more complex area than we have time to address here. But if this is an area that interests you, doing more targeted keyword searching on the topic can help you educate yourself about it.

4

Social Networking Dynamics

T'S EASY FOR JOB SEEKERS to begin to assume that the universe of jobs starts and ends online. In fact, the majority of available jobs are not posted online. In general, those in positions to hire receive a list of candidates referred to them from inside—or from within their network—before the job is even officially posted. For hiring managers, reviewing resumes from this networked pool can make their jobs easier—and if the pool happens to contain some qualified applicants, this may even preclude them from needing to sift through an abundance of resumes submitted to the public, online post. In a tough economy, this is even more likely to happen. If you've ever been frustrated by responding to a job posting the first day it appears, only to be told that it's already been filled, you know what we're talking about.

Fortunately, online networking has forever changed the dynamics of looking for a job by creating for you a "one-to-many" advantage. Instead of thinking of their activities as a *job* search, job seekers in the age of social networking must conceptualize their activities as part of an extended *people* search.

This may not seem like much of a switch, but this change in perspective alone will place you miles ahead of your competition during your job search. It also will prepare you for a long career of successful networking.

Just as salespeople are advised to always be selling, you must always be networking—even if just subtly. In this shaky economy, you might land a job tomorrow only to find yourself looking for a new job again next week.

Social Networks—What Are They?

Earlier, we alluded to the careful use of social networks, such as Facebook, in creating impressions on employers, for better or worse. Social networks attract tens and hundreds of millions of members who use them on a regular basis, many daily, others weekly or less frequently. But what are they, really?

These sites range anywhere from small social networks to massive "communities" made up of people from around the block and around the globe, with every interest imaginable—even some you haven't thought of yet!

Social networks allow you to find other people who share your interests. These may be broader, such as political leanings, religious beliefs, or a favorite soccer or football team, or they may reflect a smaller subculture, such as those who favor the Goth lifestyle, growing bonsai, or breeding Siberian huskies for show.

Social networks have profiles, pages, and groups.

Profiles allow you to put up or to "post" a profile, consisting of a page or pages about yourself, who you are, what you like—anything about yourself really—and share that information with the world or perhaps with just a select group of friends or business acquaintances.

You can have still pictures or live video of yourself, family, or events. You can add sound using audio and music files, including MP3s.

You can start a blog and build a following of kindred spirits who are interested in hearing about your life or pursuits. Likewise, you can follow others' interests through their blogs.

They can be purely informative and all business, or they can be highly entertaining or whimsical. A blog could be about your reflections on the economy, or it could be all about your fascination with insects. The only limit is your imagination.

Truly, social networks are your soapbox to advertise yourself to the world. You will need to understand how to use them in your people search and avoid embarrassing missteps along the way.

What happens on spring break or in Vegas may be funny or humorous to share with the world…but potential employers and recruiters will not be nearly as amused. As stated earlier in reference to Facebook, manage your online reputation with care.

Who Is in the Social Networks?

Although there are thousands of social networks available to you, job seekers should focus on some of the smaller, more niche-oriented, highly vertical groups that are organized around a common interest or industry.

Why Use Social Networks?

In years and decades gone by, and as recently as 30 years ago, there was no Internet. Career networking has always been "social," and that hasn't changed. It was always about "who you know."

But compared to today, networking was far more "local" than today's incredible ability to zoom around the globe in a New York minute via the Internet *AND to* reach out and to connect with an absolutely massive social network pool of people.

In days gone by, career and professional networking was restricted by the size of your immediate circle of contacts as an individual or in groups. These groups were all or mostly based in your local community.

Networking was just a tool you used when you needed a job, and it wasn't even always necessary. After you landed a job, you put networking back on the shelf until the next search. Those with a wide circle of business contacts enjoyed a substantial competitive advantage.

Traditional "candidate flow" to fill job openings depended to some extent on referrals from employees or others within your industry. But firms leaned heavily on placing classified ads in newspapers and select trade/business publications—then waited to see what flowed in. If the resume return yielded a poor quality "harvest" the process was repeated, perhaps multiple times, often lengthening the time it took to fill openings.

Social networks and social media have radically changed the mechanism of candidate flow and effected a huge expansion in the use and importance of online social networking as well as in conducting your "people search."

The more engaged you are with social networks and in using social media channels to craft/promote your "message" about what you have to offer, the more you increase your odds of a successful career search outcome.

With people changing or losing jobs far more frequently now than in the past, it is absolutely essential that you get plugged into and continually grow your own social network of contacts.

Social networks have truly opened up the candidate pool to HR departments and hiring managers as well as to third-party recruiters and headhunters. The time to locate candidates and to fill jobs has decreased dramatically.

There has been a corresponding and increasingly startling increase in the number of hiring managers and recruiters who report using social networks, such as Facebook, to source job candidates.

Utilizing social networks in recruiting also includes conduct reputation, background checking, and digging further into a candidate's background, skills, and experience—not to mention his or her choices in networking partners.

Don't be a spectator. Or, as one of our moms used to say, don't be a wallflower. Get out there and dance! Get involved. Contribute. And reap the rewards!

With a properly conceived, well executed and ongoing "people search," you can dramatically enhance your odds of obtaining a new job quickly when you are "temporarily displaced," "downsized," "rightsized," or whatever they choose to call unemployment in the future!

Selecting the Right Networks to Join and to Use

"Which are the best social networks to use?"

That's a good question with no clear-cut answer, as it depends on your definition of best.

There is an overwhelmingly large number of social networks, and new ones are being created weekly. Examples include business social network sites, more socially oriented networks sites, photo- and music-sharing social network sites, dating social network sites, highly vertical professional social network sites, and social network aggregation sites.

Each one is slightly different. And none has the same type of social network members. But just because there are many social networks, it doesn't mean that you need to join a large number of them.

To avoid information overload, start by focusing on just one or two networks. Facebook and LinkedIn are two great choices. We'll cover specific applications of these and other networks in Chapter 5, but this section provides you with the basic overview.

Once you become familiar with these two main networks, the transition to any other network will be an easy one. You will already have your content in place, so it is just a matter of making a few tweaks to accommodate the social network specifics.

Due to its focus and Fortune 500 pedigree, LinkedIn is a tremendous channel to leverage in your people search. Bear in mind, though, that you can only connect directly to people in your own personal network. No introduction is needed; just send them an "invitation." To safeguard its unique niche, to respect its members' time, and eliminate potential spamming, or UCE (unsolicited commercial e-mail), LinkedIn does not allow you to connect to people beyond your personal network.

Connecting to the contacts of one of your personal network acquaintances is highly recommended to vastly expand your personal network. These are individuals who are one time or two times removed from your personal network. You will need an "introduction" to be made on your behalf by your acquaintance to his or her contact. This helps maintain the high quality of LinkedIn's online network.

LinkedIn's features include a profile page that is customizable by adding a head-shot image, personal/business information, e-mail address, and other relevant information. Users can seek endorsements from past clients or colleagues who are willing to provide testimonials on their behalf. This is a great way to build your credibility and to have potential recruiters, employers, and consultants learn more about you.

Groups within LinkedIn will provide you with the ability to research and to join specific groups of interest around product/services, markets/industries, or other focal points. This, too, is a great way to expand your presence/brand and to network via people searching.

The "Answers" feature within LinkedIn offers the ability to pose questions to your network if you are looking for solutions to a business problem or market research. These questions are posed and e-mailed only to your personal network, and you have the ability to mail to all or to be selective about who will receive your message. This also enables you to reply to questions you receive from others in your network, and it's a fabulous tool for positioning yourself by adding value and demonstrating your willingness to help and to offer solutions to others.

NOTE: Do not use this vehicle to "sell" or to "solicit" business. This is a surefire way to isolate yourself from the very network that can help you. The business that does come your way will arrive more indirectly as a result of your "contributions" in asking/answering questions and providing value.

By inviting others to join your network, you can increase your network of professional contacts and broaden your connections exponentially. You can identify potential connections via LinkedIn's search functionality.

The other place to start with social media is Facebook. We'll go into greater detail on Facebook in the next chapter, but let's take a quick look at it here. Facebook is the largest online social networking site and one of the Internet's most trafficked destinations.

When many people think of Facebook, they envision it as the place where college students post photos from parties and attempt to hook up with romantic partners. However, this social networking site is now a dynamo that has been increasingly embraced by individuals over 25. Today it is a viable place for professionals to network with the ultimate goal of finding their next jobs. So despite their high number of younger users, don't look down on Facebook or MySpace, which is another of the "Big Four" social networking sites. Recruiters and HR mine these huge pools of social communities every day, looking for candidates for their job assignments.

Why ignore such a potentially rich source of contacts that can help you in many different ways? Whereas LinkedIn is more business focused, Facebook and MySpace are just the opposite. They emphasize the "social" component of the phrase "social media."

That means you will need to be more deliberate when setting up your profile if you're new to these sites. You also should consider modifying your profile if you're a current member to take a more professional approach with it. You may wish to forgo filling out certain sections that make it seem too personal (e.g., relationship status, interested in, favorite books/movies).

We're not suggesting that you should eliminate your personal side; we don't think that's advisable. You want some personal aspects so as to demonstrate your authenticity as a qualified individual. Also, letting part of "you" show through helps make you more multidimensional. Noting some of your unique interests, hobbies, and pursuits can help others make more of a "connection" with you. These qualities can humanize you. It's always easier to write off a candidate who is no more than a name on a page along with some job experiences as opposed to someone who comes off as a real person.

Let's face it: People hire people, not profiles. This is what makes informational meetings so important. They enable you to explore career opportunities and to learn about those who are working in an industry or company you might like to enter. Although social networking can make connecting all the more efficient, it still doesn't replace the face-to-face meeting. So don't be shy about inviting those you admire for a quick cup of coffee—your treat!

We'll go into much more detail on the "Big Four" social networking sites in the next chapter.

Build Trust through Adding Value

So once you have begun to build profiles and to make connections through such sites as Facebook and LinkedIn, in what specific ways can you "add value" or help your new social network contacts as you work to befriend them and to gain their trust?

Below are 21 ideas to get you started. We're certain you will come up with at least another 21 by applying these to your own situation and expanding on them. The key is to think creatively. What would make you feel appreciated? What would make you take notice of someone in a sea of strangers? Here are some starting points for individuals you will encounter:

1. Give a personal testimonial about them, their work, or their business.
2. Review and mention a book they wrote.
3. Make them aware of a white paper you saw that could be of interest.
4. Tell them how much you enjoyed a particular blog post of theirs.
5. Comment on the clean look and attention-getting design of their Web site.
6. Compliment them on something they've said, done, or achieved.
7. Drop them a congratulatory note about a speech they made or seminar they conducted.
8. Mention them and their product/service to others in your social network(s).
9. Give them some free publicity in the form of a "plug" on your blog or Web site.
10. Send them a potential business lead.
11. Let them know of a competitive situation in their business that could help them.
12. Mail or e-mail them a copy of a recent promotion you saw about them with a short handwritten "Congrats!"
13. Recommend a book you read that might be of interest.
14. Turn them on to a timely article you read online or offline.
15. Send them an e-mail with a link to the article.
16. Snail mail them a copy of the article.

17. Congratulate them on a 10-year—or whatever year—work anniversary.
18. Compliment them on their good-looking family, if you saw a picture of them together.
19. Send them some information on one of their hobbies if you saw mention of it in an article.
20. Congratulate them on a major project completion that you read about in a trade magazine.
21. Comment on a new innovation or invention they just had mentioned.

The key in all of this is to be yourself. Be sincere and genuine. In this age of authenticity, you must mean what you say and follow through. And you must learn to really care. Only then will you build the necessary, deep trust and credibility in others' eyes, and in their view of you.

Establish this trust, and regularly stay in touch, and you'll make true online social network friends you can count on—not just for your next job, but for life.

Exploiting the One-to-Many Approach to Finding a Job

First, we must remind you that we're not suggesting that you abandon the traditional ways of looking for a job.

As any good marketer knows—and that's what you are, a marketer of yourself—it's never smart to make assumptions about what works and what doesn't. Rather, the ideal approach is to test everything and to see what works for you.

If going to real-world networking events gets you the gig, then so be it. If finding a job in the newspaper classified section does it for you—kudos! The goal of using social networking for job search is to give you more options—more job-hunting tactics to test.

And the new tactic of using social networks to speed up your job search is highly leverageable. In other words, you can get a lot more mileage out of a little bit of invested time and energy relative to traditional job-hunting tactics.

Instead of telling your story by sending your resume to one person or company at a time, social networks allow you to broadcast your message using the one-to-many approach.

As we mentioned briefly in Chapter 3, traditional methods of job hunting, such as applying through newspaper or online job listings, can best be thought of as using a one-to-one approach. You are reaching out with one resume to one job at one specific employer.

Conversely, social networks, such as Facebook, MySpace, LinkedIn, and others, are best thought of as platforms that will enable you to establish ongoing one-to-many relationships.

Therefore, you prepare your message—or better yet *versions* of your message in the form of resumes—and then you can start building relationships with a greater number of people simultaneously.

You're not laboriously sending resumes out one at a time to someone who might give you a job. Instead, we're going to show you how to blast your message out there—in a targeted way—to people who might give you a job directly or help you find one indirectly by passing your information on to others who can hire you.

We show you how to grow your network quickly, starting with your own personal group of contacts (your friends and business acquaintances) and then expanding that circle to the contacts of those individuals, as well as building networks around recruiters, employers, and other target audiences.

Start with this people-centric perspective, and you're on your way to understanding how to best utilize social networks to get your next job.

Versioning

In the previous chapter, we talked briefly about versioning. As with the example we gave with Susan (a schoolteacher mulling a career change) there are times when a candidate might be wise to prepare a variety of messages—and resumes—that are tailored to the needs and interests of different employment niches.

For example, we know one professional who was planning a career change several years ago. One strength and weakness that he faced as a candidate was that he had done many different things and was open to pursuing a wide variety of job options. While this greatly increased the number of opportunities that were available to him, it also created a challenge for him as well. If he were to present himself as "all things to all people," he may well have come across as someone who was way too broad and unfocused to fit in the narrow confines of a given job description.

So what did he do? He created three fairly different versions of his resume. He called one his consulting resume, and it focused on his flexibility and creativity in handling various creative projects for high-profile clients. His second was his educator resume, and the slant of his job description on that resume highlighted work he had done as a teacher, instructional designer, and stand-up presenter. His third resume was his manager resume, and that one showcased experiences with supervising, managing, and collaborating with co-workers and other organizations.

He even varied his "Interests" section on each resume. Each featured honest interests, but specific passions were included or omitted depending on the audience.

Obviously, creating multiple resumes can be a great deal of work, and you need to have a system of keeping track of who has received which resume. That said, it can be a helpful concept for those considering multiple career paths simultaneously.

People Search versus Job Search

With social networks, your primary focus is not looking for a job or job openings. Your initial, main objectives are to (1) locate, (2) connect to, and (3) build relationships with an ever-widening network of individuals.

There are a variety of methods that you can employ to this end. We walk you through many of these in greater detail later, but let's hit some basics now.

Your secondary—and ultimate—objective in the people-search process is to identify job/career opportunities. Sure, this is your obvious goal, but if you begin with the more subtle main objective of connecting to a broad range of individuals instead of just narrowly focusing on those who might be able to give you a job, you will start to see that it's the smarter strategy. It will open up many more doors faster, significantly expand your options, and enable you to find the right job more easily than the more traditional job-hunting methods.

You can choose to take the time to learn new, more effective strategies, which might make you a little uncomfortable at first. Alternatively, you can stay in your comfort zone, blindly sending your resumes to jobs via Monster.com and HotJobs.com to compete with all those people who are doing the same because it's relatively easy and mindless.

Naturally, it's always best to zig while others are zagging. Stop job hunting and start people hunting!

If you make the commitment to change the way you approach looking for a job, not only will it help you find a better job faster, it will also be a smart, long-term investment that will pay you regular dividends throughout your professional life.

The idea behind using social networking for a job search is to grow your little backyard garden, meaning your limited circle of current contacts, into an ever-expanding farm—the massive network of contacts that can sustain you for the rest of your life.

You must plant, cultivate, and harvest on an ongoing basis rather than taking time to grow your farm and then simply abandoning the harvest.

As noted earlier, it is almost a guarantee that you will be back in the job market several more times over your life. On average, today's employees will hold an average of seven different jobs over their lifetimes—and this number shows signs of increasing as the economy continues to stagnate.

Hence, the best advice is to play it smart. Start creating a foundation now instead of having to start over from square one next time you have to find a job. Those who have followed this advice report that when they found themselves in need of a job, their networks were there—ready and willing to help them get back to work. We'd like you to have this type of a network at your disposal, too.

Contact Your Core

Once you have created your list of potential employers, you will need to cull this list to your "Top 10" list. Having more than 10 will not only feel overwhelming to you, it will show a lack of focus to those with whom you might share these company names.

We are not advocating that you restrict your search to just 10 companies to the exclusion of all others, but as your core focus, a list of 10 is plenty.

Once you have your Top 10 list ready to go, reach out to your close existing base of contacts. Let them know your situation as well as what sort of opportunity you're seeking, and specifically ask if they have connections to people who may work in your Top 10 list of firms.

If your contacts know of any opportunities, even better. Your primary objective is to see if they can identify any contacts inside your Top 10 list, and, if so, if they might be willing to make an introduction so that you might expand your social network contact base in a targeted fashion. Once you have this peer-generated start, you can then begin to build a relationship.

If your immediate circle comes up empty-handed, use search engines to find employees who currently work in your Top 10 companies. With more than 130 million blogs on the Technorati Web site, try searching them to identify someone who works at one of the companies you have targeted. In addition, search corporate pages, groups that may have a public-facing presence, Facebook, and Twitter using keyword searches.

NOTE: While you're at it, search for blogs that have job banks, and subscribe to these feeds. One recent trend, particularly for larger blogs, is to begin integrating job banks using back-end software, such as Jobamatic.com. This can be another helpful source for finding jobs based on your interest or industry.

Once you have identified some names from your friends or through searches, reach out and connect with them. Social media offers the wonderful advantage of breaking down barriers and leveling barriers to access. Within the bounds of social graces and understanding how relationships are built, job seekers can now message individuals with whom they have had no previous connection. Candidates who have done their homework and determined the most appropriate channel for contact, such as LinkedIn, Facebook, or even a direct e-mail, can share their interest in the company, and, if properly executed, begin to get to know individuals within the target companies.

We go into greater detail into the specifics of how to create and to leverage your group of Top 10 employers in Chapter 6.

Overcoming Hurdles

There may be some concerns that you have been mulling over as you read this. Here are some typical objections that tend to arise:

"That's all well and good—reaching out to new potential contacts, and providing value—but outreach is simply not my strength."

"I'd like to be able to network effectively, but when it comes to networking, I am nothing short of introverted."

"I'm just not comfortable with talking to people outside those I know well. I'm not good at selling like other people are."

For those of you who are introverted or slightly shy, online social networking has a major advantage over traditional face-to-face networking: There is no immediate face-to-face meeting to affect your nerves.

You absolutely should attend business networking events in your area that may be of help in your search, as challenging as this may be for those who are social caterpillars rather than social butterflies. But if you feel at all intimidated about reaching out personally or via e-mail, here are a few tips:

- How would you act and approach a networking situation if you weren't shy? Trying practicing this with close friends and see how you do. Keep in mind that all behavior is learned, and it all can be changed.
- Work at being genuinely interested in others. This helps move the focus away from you and onto others. Also, most people like to talk about themselves.
- Other people—more than you may suspect—feel just as uncomfortable as you. Think of how you can help put them more at ease, and then do it.
- Ask or offer something—a question, an observation, a compliment—and then simply listen. Focus on that person's response with a genuine interest, and then reply accordingly.

Of course, some of these ideas are slightly easier in person versus in an online setting. But stretch your imagination to see how you can apply them online. Here are a few great questions you can use in an online setting or e-mail, if the right opportunity occurs:

- "If I happen across (a contact, a deal, an opportunity, etc.), what would the ideal referral be for you?"
- "What's your biggest challenge?"

Listen to the answer and see if you can offer a contact, suggestion, or some sort of help. Even if you can't provide assistance today, make a note so that when you do, you can. It shows that you're interested in *them* and WANT TO *help*. People appreciate that. Remember—give before you get!

Getting Introduced and Referred

This is probably the hardest part of social networking for many people to learn.

Asking for advice, asking for help, and asking for an introduction to someone else's friend or valuable contact often strikes job seekers as a challenge.

Ironically, this is probably most true for those in the sales and business development profession. If you sell and close deals for a living, having a conversation and helping someone without the focus of an "ending" may feel a bit unnatural. But building trust and doing for others first is the foundation that you need to lay before constructing a network that will give back to you.

As with any foundation, the more you can build a base of relationships that is solid, strong, and large, the more you will be able to construct a large and complex structure of individuals who will be ready and willing to give back when the opportunity arises.

The Warmer, the Better

It is always far easier and much more productive, regardless of objective, to get a "warm" referral or introduction to someone than trying to get an audience by approaching someone directly.

In the sales business, professions refer to a "cold call." Ice cold. With a direct cold-call approach, there is no prior relationship, no common ground, no mutual interest or frame of reference, no mutual acquaintance or friend. Even more importantly, there is no reason to talk to you.

It's how the Law of Large Numbers theory works: Throw enough mud on the wall, and perhaps some small amount of it will stick. In a job search, this is equivalent to sending out 100 resumes to a broad array of jobs with a generic cover letter. These are the first candidates to be eliminated.

In the world of social networking, the best results come not from plowing through as many contacts as you can but from building relationships that will lead to "warm" introductions to the people and organizations you want to target.

Get into the Group

If you want to find out what's going on in an industry and troll for new contacts, a great idea is to harness the power of a shared interest or community: groups.

Once again, the search engines can be a great source of information. Both Google and Yahoo! have large numbers of these groups. Simply type in "Google Groups" or "Yahoo! Groups" into a search bar, and start poking around to find one or more that may have some of the types of people you are seeking. Some groups may have a few dozen members, and some may have many thousands. Each group has a little blurb about its focus or interests, so this makes it easier for you to determine if joining and contributing may be helpful to your overall search.

Share your Top 10 with your network. Ask for help with leads, including names of people who might be in positions to assist, as well as job openings.

Beyond Networking...Friendworking

Even before the advent of social technologies, people searched for connections. We all tend to befriend people who are like us, such as people who share the same worldview or hobbies or interests. Today's social media world has simply expanded our ability to do so to an exponential degree.

Social networks speed up the meeting-and-greeting process by providing technologies that allow you to connect or to reconnect with those who have interests, skills, or experiences in common. At least some amount of face-to-face networking has been replaced by online networking.

Yet the exercise is the same. It's all about making the social connection. You may have more luck finding a job through alumni of the schools, colleges, or universities you attended, because there will be an instant natural connection.

Those who do the hiring in companies will often admit that they hired a candidate because they liked and trusted that individual due to some connection. Product marketers spend billions each year trying to convince consumers that the people who use their products or services are like them. They try to build empathy and trust with their target audiences, because they know that will increase the likelihood that someone will become a buyer.

Your Quick Label

Although creating the expanded, in-depth version of your personal brand is important, it's equally as important to consider shorter-form content. That is, in the lightning-fast, short-attention-span online world, coupled with the generally frantic pace of business today, you may only have 10 seconds—or one line—to summarize who you are and what you do. So you'll need to prepare for this.

We call this your *Quick Label*.

This is your quick broadcast message. It's the bait that hopefully will hook some people long enough to get them thinking about what you can do for your next employer.

Later in this book, we focus on the Problem, Action, Results, or "PAR," formula, because using it will differentiate you from your competitors in the job-search process. Most people will just focus on themselves, whereas you are going to focus on what you can do for the cmopany through having the service mentality that the PAR formula will force you to think through.

For now, though, let's focus on a more basic message, the Quick Label.

There are four key points that you must cover quickly. This is not to say that you should limit yourself to these four points. Circumstances may require you to go beyond these four, but it's important to keep your Quick Label short and to the point. In essence, you will want to center on four key points:

1. Your Main Role
Although you may resist the idea of labeling yourself or putting yourself in a box, your priority while looking for a job is to communicate your message as quickly and clearly as possible. Your main role is how others might categorize you and should convey how you

would fit into any business organization.

For example, you might be a marketing executive, business development executive, accountant, financial analyst, or human resources specialist. In one or two words, you should be able to communicate your main organizational role.

You might have different Quick Labels in different settings. Maybe you have experience in both sales and marketing, in which case you might just say that you are a sales and marketing executive. You might be a recruiter who would like to make a transition toward a training and development role. It's okay to be more than one thing. But don't try to list all your skills in your main role.

2. Areas of Expertise

Your main role might already cover your areas of expertise by default, but, if appropriate, you can elaborate a bit on some additional skills.

In this second part of your Quick Label, you might also mention the industries in which you've worked. Again, if you are communicating with someone in a health-care organization, there might be no need to mention that you've also done accounting for an information technology company. You make the call.

Generally, though, if you are at the very beginning of your job-hunting campaign, you might mention all the industries in which you've worked. You might not want to come off as a job hopper, but you may wish to cast your net a bit wider at first and then tighten your message as you get into situations where it is obvious that you should focus your presentation on a specific industry or set of skills.

3. Who You Help

Just as you will want to mention relevant industries, you'll also want to give a sense of the type and size of organizations that have employed you. Have you worked for start-ups? Large global corporations? Government organizations? Not-for-profit organizations?

If it's true, it might be a good idea to mention that you've worked for companies of various sizes. This shows that you can be successful in an entrepreneurial environment or a bureaucratic setting. Flexibility and a broad range of experience is highly valued in today's fast-moving job market.

4. Pains You Solve

Here's where you are going to give shorter versions of the "Problem" element of the PAR formula, which we expand on later.

Here are some examples:

- "I help Internet start-ups that are wrestling with how to plan and to execute effective digital marketing strategies."
- "I work with health-care companies that need to streamline their accounting systems to cut costs and to increase productivity."
- "I consult with financial institutions on how to motivate their salespeople so they can sell more and sell faster."

These are only suggestions. You might be comfortable with a different way of presenting yourself. Whichever style you prefer, be sure that you cover the basics succinctly. This will ensure that others will know what you do and be able to pass you on to an appropriate contact—or hire you if you happen to meet the needs of their organization.

JOB SEEKER SUCCESS STORY:
Work Your Network

Stephen Kohnle is continuing his job search through social networking sites after being "downsized" as director of worldwide sales for a small technology company.

Kohnle, who documented his ongoing search in a column for *Business Week* magazine, says contacts in his network have proved to be invaluable resources while searching for a new position.

He attributes personal, and now online, networking to his success in getting the jobs he has sought during the last 25 years. Although the art of networking has changed with the technology, Kohnle believes that you need "more than a handful of contacts" and experience in the field to get a good job.

"Job seekers want to stand out in a crowd, especially one filled with others eyeing similar positions," Kohnle says. "This is where social media can be a powerful tool."

Kohnle started his search by exploring his LinkedIn network contacts and the various industries they worked in that interested him. He then started researching companies in those industries to find some he would want to apply to.

He expanded his search through the Twitter status updating site to follow people who might help his search so he could market his skills to them. Through sharing "tweets" with these people, Kohnle could share resources and respond to their interests and questions.

This new medium, Kohnle believes, helps potential candidates "stand out" from the rest of the pack, as many job seekers are only sending e-mail applications and resumes to every job posting they see. Getting noticed by employers is "the name of the game," according to Kohnle.

SOURCE: Kohnle, Stephen. "Social Media and the Job Search Editorial." *Business Week*, 13 July 2009 <http://www.businessweek.com/bwdaily/dnflash/content/jul2009/db20090710_159348.htm>.

Balancing Long-Term Versus Short-Term

As you start building your online circle of contacts in Facebook, LinkedIn, and other social networks, you will begin to develop different levels of contacts. Consider these as concentric circles, like a dartboard, with your immediate friends and family as the bull's-eye. Then you'll be adding layers of circles as you expand your network from there.

Naturally, your relationships with individuals in the outer circles will not be as frequent or intimate as those you have with people you've known and loved for years. Of course, part of your strategy is to increase the number of people with whom you have deeper relationships. You will want to identify people who are able and willing to help you, and getting to that point in a relationship can take time.

Those with whom you have more casual relationships are more susceptible to falling out of touch, but, of course, you don't have all the time in the world to keep in touch with everyone you meet. Hence, you'll need to be able to pick and to choose key players who have broad networks that can help you later.

If this sounds a bit Machiavellian, bear in mind that this is all about strategy and being efficient with your limited time in order to get back into the workforce as rapidly as possible. You also should absolutely be prepared to help other contacts when possible in the future.

Naturally you want to secure your next job right away. And your core group of closest contacts can be very helpful in quickly directing you to a few select opportunities. By all means, go after the low-hanging fruit by reaching out to them first and letting them know that you're looking.

But keep in mind that you'll need to work on two distinct yet related tracks. Slowly but steadily build longer-term relationship, while also looking for the current next job. After all, you'll be looking for another "next job" down the road, so you'll need to start the process now.

Don't Burn Bridges Before They're Built

We've touched on the importance of building relationships within your social network before leveraging new contacts in a job search. Let's drill down into a few more specifics on this front.

Remember that social networks are first and foremost *social*. They're not business networks. If you cut to the chase too early, you'll end up turning people off and getting nowhere fast.

Consider this: Are you most inclined to help (a) someone you know and like or (b) someone you don't like or hardly know? Sales are all about forging relationships in which people like and trust you. For the purpose of finding a job, social networking functions in the same way.

Have you ever been on the receiving end of a message from someone you don't know who launched directly into some variation on *"I'm looking for new job and so-and-so said you could help me? My background is blah, blah, blah; I have a degree in X and am looking for 'Y'"*? If so, we doubt that you were delighted. Most busy people will simply delete such an email from a stranger. If you are one of those kind souls who felt compelled to send a reply, chances are it was probably something fairly short, impersonal yet courteous, along the lines of *"I don't know of anything, but if I do hear of something, I'll keep you in mind."*

The vast majority of the times the full-frontal assault simply doesn't work. It's a one-and-done way of approaching a relationship. In short, this is relationship-building suicide.

If you move too quickly, you run the risk of not only missing an opportunity with a newfound contact. You also may jeopardize your relationship with the person who referred you to the new contact initially. That person you contacted might forward your desperate e-mail to your friend along with a derisive comment. This is a lose/lose outcome.

For more on developing stellar relationships, we recommend Dale Carnegie's classic, *How to Win Friends and Influence People* or Stephen Covey's *The Seven Habits of Highly Effective People*. In fact, Covey's fifth habit, "Seek First to Understand, THEN to Be Understood," has a corollary as it relates to job search: "Seek First to Help as You Build a Relationship, THEN to Ask for Help."

So get to know your new contacts to some extent first. Know more than just their first names. Know something personal about them, and try to find common interests that may lead to a solid relationship.

Social networks help you do that, because people fill their profiles with personal information about themselves. Knowing how to use this information will help you build relationships faster—by finding common bonds, like interests, and so forth. This can lead to you a job—maybe sooner, maybe later.

5

Social Networks:
The "Big Four"

CYBER SOCIAL NETWORKING is the new cocktail party, so you'll need to know how to work the room. You are representing Y.O.U., Inc.

As we discussed earlier, you need to think of yourself as a brand, just like Coca-Cola. You want to spread awareness of your name, image, abilities, and individuality into the consciousness of anyone who is a potential customer for your services. You can accomplish this enormous task while wearing fuzzy bunny slippers with mouse in hand and a social network on your computer screen.

All it takes is every spare moment you have.

"I think every individual is now an entrepreneur in terms of the business of themselves," says Reid Hoffman, founder of LinkedIn, the go-to corporate networking site. "It's how they get their next job opportunity, how they get a promotion. All of that comes from how they manage the network around them."

This 21st-century phenomenon proves Hungarian writer Frigyes Karinthy's theory that anyone on the planet can be connected to any other person by six links or "six degrees of separation." It is *your* job to follow the trail of crumbs to get to those people who will open their doors and invite you in.

According to the U.S. Bureau of Labor Statistics, 15.3 million Americans were unemployed at the end of 2009. Remember the adage, "It's not what you know, but who you know"? It's been upgraded to "It's what you know, who you know, *and* who your friends know."

The popularity and power of social connectivity on the Internet is astounding. From 2008 to 2009, the number of people using Facebook increased 666 percent, while the number of MySpace users declined by 31 percent, and LinkedIn users rose 69 percent.[1] Its probability and outcome: more users, more connections; more connections, more opportunities.

More than one billion people use social networking. LinkedIn members alone include every Fortune 500 Company and even the president of the United States. How's that for a connection?

Get connected and take advantage of the best, easiest, and least-expensive job-hunting system to ever emerge. Take a breath, and we'll make our way through the social networking maze.

Get the lay of the land. Visit each site—Facebook.com, MySpace. com and LinkedIn.com—and get a feel for what they have to offer. Be patient, because it can initially be confusing. Pick the site that best fits your goals. Once you root around for a bit, you'll discover the others are simply variations on the theme.

If you already have a Facebook or MySpace page, start cleaning house. According to a recent survey by CareerBuilder.com, 45 percent of employers use social networking sites to research job

---

[1] "Time Spent on Facebook up 700 Percent, but MySpace.com Still Tops for Video, According to Nielsen" 2 June, 2009. http://en-us.nielsen.com/main/news/news_releases/2009/june/time_on_facebook

candidates. Breaking it down: 29 percent of employers look for you on Facebook, 26 percent on LinkedIn and 21 percent on MySpace.

Look at your page, your videos, your photographs, and your emoticons; those happy faces could cost you an interview. Make sure you're comfortable with the groups you've joined. And check your list of friends, because a prospective employer probably will. Guilt by association may not be fair, but it happens all the time. Look at your page through the eyes of a potential employer (or your mom). Check for inappropriate language and photos—regardless of who did the posting. Remember those bachelor party photos or the one of you frolicking in the snow with only your skis to keep you warm? Delete, delete, delete.

A CareerBuilder.com 2009 survey cited the following reasons potential candidates were rejected for employment:

- Posting provocative or inappropriate information or photographs: 53 percent
- Posting information about drinking or drug use: 44 percent
- Badmouthing a previous employer, clients, or co-workers: 35 percent
- Poor communication skills: 29 percent
- Making discriminatory comments: 29 percent
- Lying about qualifications: 24 percent
- Sharing proprietary information about a previous employer: 20 percent

Remember, you are a professional. What you write must exude professionalism and have pristine grammar, perfect spelling, and no typos. Spell-check it and recheck it, remembering that spellcheckers won't be able to tell you if you've used "their" when you should've used "they're" or "affect" when you meant "effect." Read it out loud before you hit "Send."

JOB SEEKER SUCCESS STORY:
Relocating and Jobless? Let LinkedIn Be Your Welcome Wagon.

Chuck Hester of Raleigh, North Carolina, used profiles on Facebook, Twitter, and LinkedIn extensively in helping him get a job in 2008.

Hester, an information technology specialist, needed a job after relocating with his family from California. It proved to be a daunting task, because he was in unfamiliar territory when attempting to make inroads into the business marketplace in his new home.

He started his search by using his accumulated 500 contacts on the LinkedIn professional networking site to get the word out about his move in order to reach marketing professionals in the Raleigh area. A high-ranking executive for an e-mail software company called iContact responded to Hester and hired him as the corporate communications director for the company.

Hester was surprised at how quickly his social networking skills yielded positive results. He still uses the sites and sends messages to contacts as he travels so they can meet up informally for dinner or drinks. One of these meetings in the San Francisco area brought 20 people from his network together.

He also organizes a more formal meeting every other month for those in his contact database. Those "LinkedIn Live" functions generate between 50 and 200 members. Members attending include job candidates, recruiters, and executives.

Hester says he could track 20 to 30 people who became employed just from attending these networking events.

He likens the experience to digging a well before you get thirsty so the resource is there when you need it.

SOURCE: Rosenbloom, Stephanie. "Looking for Work on Facebook." *New York Times,* 1 May 2008 <http://www.nytimes.com/2008/05/01/fashion/01networking.html>.

Go ahead and Google your name to see what pops up. You don't want any unpleasant surprises to rear their ugly heads during an interview.

Now that you've cleansed your sites, it's time to ask yourself some hard questions: Who am I? What are my core values? Where do I see myself in five years (a very common question asked in an interview)? Am I willing to relocate, and, perhaps most importantly, what do I want from a job?

All these must be clear to you before you can communicate them to the world, so give that exercise some thought. Make notes.

Facebook

Facebook came to be in February 2004, originally as an idea by a student to organize and to aggregate a "facebook" of personal photos of Harvard University students. From that modest beginning, Facebook has grown into the Google of social networks.

"Massive" doesn't begin to describe this network's huge social networking membership user base. Among social networking sites, Facebook is the indisputable leader with more than 350 million active users.[2] At its heart, it is *the* site for finding friends, classmates, and those love 'em or hate 'em blasts from the past. In April 2009, Facebook CEO Mark Zuckerman confirmed that the site had crashed the 200-million member mark, registering over 100 million monthly visits to its Web site.

As the numbers illustrate, a larger percentage of its users represents a younger slice of the population. Approximately 65 percent of Facebook members are under the age of 35, and approximately 40 percent are in 18- to 24-year-old age bracket.

---

[2] Facebook: 300 million active users, "Free Cash-Flow Positive" 15 September 2009. http://www.insidefacebook.com/2009/09/15/facebook-reaches-300-million-monthly-active-users/

However, an interesting shift has been occurring since spring of 2008. Facebook has experienced a dramatic uptick of new members in the 35- to 54-year-old demographic, which now represents approximately 17 percent of total users.

This segment grew at a rate of approximately 200 percent in 2008 before accelerating to an even faster growth rate of 260 percent in 2009. That 17 percent equals more than 30 million users in this more-mature career professional market segment.

That should be of keen interest to you in your people search. Even though the majority of Facebook users would not likely represent a majority of corporate hiring managers, 17 percent of that group belongs to that cohort, and that number will continue to grow. You do want to tap into that segment and build relationships with those individuals.

Not only that, but the two-thirds of Facebook users who are under age 35—many tens of millions of people—certainly could work for many of the firms that you might be interested in working for, too. Those individuals could be ideal entry points into their network of contacts, and those contacts could help your efforts considerably.

Within the Facebook platform, job seekers can take advantage of two main ways of acquiring a job. Facebook Marketplace lists job openings in a user's network, and the job seeker can message the hiring manager directly. In addition, job seekers can join groups and fan pages to find people with like interests and begin to engage with them.

Tactically, go to "Groups" on your Facebook home page, and in the search field, type in the keyword "jobs." Enter your profession in the new search field, and you'll get a list of related jobs. Depending on your search term, you may be directed to a list of job sites, such as Monster.com.

Also under "Groups," use the keyword specific to your career choice, such as "accounting." There you'll find several job sites. Choose one, click on "original post," and you'll find detailed information on that specific job. Some links may be vague, but keep searching and you may get lucky. For more creative types, such as designers and writers, there'll be sites that connect you with jobs and support groups. But you may also find a community of frustrated job seekers, complete with whining. But perhaps it's comforting to know you're not alone out there.

For a more targeted approach, you may choose to advertise using Facebook social ads.

As a sidebar, if you are going to take the advertising route, you should try Google's AdWords advertising platform, in which you can explore cost-per-click or cost-per-impression pricing for advertisements on Google or its myriad AdWords partner sites.

Before creating advertisements in any space, job seekers must first create a landing page. If you have already created a Web site or blog, you may choose to use this existing site as the click-through to your resume page.

The content of your ad should be carefully constructed. You will want to include a title in which you position yourself as an expert or specialist in your field. Include your top accomplishments in five or six words and a few key descriptors. Also include links in your ad to all relevant social network profiles in addition to your primary URL.

The advantage to Facebook's social ads is that they allow job seekers to utilize Facebook's newsfeed to send your ad through your network of friends.

If you're not inclined to post a social ad, Facebook contains other means of seeking out employment. For example, on the home page, click on "Pages" on the navigation bar at the top, and then search "Hiring." This will take you to site administrators who are looking for businesses to post their jobs or friends to share jobs they've heard about. However, these pages are vague and difficult to navigate. Searching "Now Hiring" leads to some niche sites postings jobs in fields ranging from the sublime to the ridiculous. These range from the traditional, such as health-care, to the "too good to be true," such as getting paid to go to nightclubs. These pages however, are not updated very often and are fairly useless. Play around with the search terms, and see what you get.

Another effective way to use Facebook to find a job is to let your friends know you're seeking employment. Post your resume. Naturally, this is only applicable if you're unemployed; you don't want to alert your current employer that you're job hunting.

Post links to sites outside Facebook that offer news and information related to your field. BNET.com is a great example. Doing this lets everyone know you keep up to date on the information relating to your line of work. Another benefit comes when a friend hears of a job and thinks of you because you're always posting. That's when TOMA—Top of the Mind Awareness—kicks in. And you want to be on top. Right?

Expand your "brand" by posting an ad or creating a fan page. On the left side of the home page, click "Ads" and "Pages." If you create a page, you'll be asked into which category you fit (e.g., artist, product, organization). Click "Create Page," and begin by writing about your subject. From there, post your work, blog, invite people to become fans, or start a new thread (discussion to which people post replies). Everything you do to keep your name alive helps boost the brand that is Y.O.U., Inc.

MySpace

The MySpace slogan, "A Place for Friends," is indicative of its mission. On the home page you'll find, "Today on MySpace," which features celebrity updates, music, and videos targeted to an audience of 20-somethings. It makes sense, considering 60percent of its over 70 million users are less than 25 years of age.[3]

The MySpace focus is on friends, blogging, dating, instant messaging, checking out bands, and the posting of sometimes entertaining but very low-budget short films and karaoke videos— some of which are excellent, by the way. If you have hopes of your video or garage band going viral and landing a great gig, this could be your dream come true. But MySpace doesn't seem to be the place for corporate job seekers. If you type "jobs" into the search field on the home page, you'll see jobs you never knew *were* jobs. Actually, it's an amusing romp—but not necessarily where you want to spend your precious job-seeking time.

MySpace allows the creation of a home page that reflects your personality. Post your videos, favorite music, and links to favorite Web sites. Start a discussion by asking a question, such as "What was the best job you've ever had?" You may get interesting answers and could possibly connect with someone who's hiring in your field.

LinkedIn

With 11 million unique visitors[4] all looking for the same thing, LinkedIn is for the hardcore job seeker. This is where the six degrees

[3] Social Media Site Demographics. 11 February, 2009.
http://e-strategyblog.com/2009/02/social-networking-site-demographics/
[4] Facebook: 300 million active users, "Free Cash-Flow Positive" 15 September 2009.
http://www.insidefacebook.com/2009/09/15/facebook-reaches-300-million-monthly-active-users/

of separation rule is most evident. The unspoken rule here is, "You use me, and I'll use you."

LinkedIn has been touted as the number-one place for job seekers—with approximately 35 million users, including recruiters. Recruiters use LinkedIn as a convenient means of sourcing potential candidates. Most job seekers, however, fail to optimize their LinkedIn profiles and thus may be missing some key opportunities.

Job seekers must ensure that their profile pages are complete. Ideally, they should join and participate in groups, exchange endorsements with peers, and secure recommendations from clients or colleagues. They should post professional photos (ideally, the same photos used across all other social networking profiles). Simply put, a complete profile gives any job seeker the upper hand.

When using LinkedIn to search for a job, you should first explore your own network to determine who from your core group might help you get to the hiring managers of your selected companies. Remember that you are not limited to your first-degree connections. LinkedIn lists first-, second-, and third-degree connections: Use them all to find an opening. And don't forget to import your contacts from Gmail and Outlook to rapidly broaden your first-degree connections.

So, now that you're in LinkedIn, how can it work for job search? Here's a broad but pared-down example: Norman is an unemployed attorney with impressive credentials and myriad business associates. He has a killer summary, an excellent profile, and a professional headshot. One by one, he seeks out his contacts and requests they link to his network. They do. His network begins to grow. He takes advantage of LinkedIn's listing of people he may know. This is right on his home page, and it changes each time he logs in. He invites them, too. Meanwhile, he asks his connections to recommend him.

They do, and the recommendations are posted on his profile page, along with recommendations he has made for others.

The more recommendations he has, the more his name comes up in searches. Also, on his home page, he goes to the scroll-down bar and under "Contacts," chooses "Network Statistics." He types in lawyers, and every profile with the word "lawyer" in it is listed. This is one of Norman's favorite features.

He organizes a group of similar career-minded members and grows his network. It eventually swells to 500, and he keeps in contact with as many as possible. He says it's time-consuming but worth it. He also takes advantage of the list of available jobs reflective of his career, listed conveniently on his home page.

Norman is a perfect example of a LinkedIn success story. Because of his tenacity and talent, he lands an interview with a prestigious law firm.

Social networking is a commitment, and it needs to be taken seriously. Be vigilant. Don't go a single day without checking in. Ask one more person to join your network. Request or make one more recommendation. While looking for a job, consider social networking your temporary full-time job. If you work it right, Facebook, LinkedIn and MySpace will allow you to replace that all-consuming can't-pay-my-bills stress with the kind of stress that comes with a paycheck.

When you're ready to start your profile, go the LinkedIn home page, then to "Profile," then to "Edit." One of the first things you'll be asked is to summarize your professional life—to put your past, present and hopes for the future into one or two paragraphs. This is the introduction to Y.O.U., Inc., as a brand.

Start writing. Don't be afraid to ask for help. This may be daunting, but it's doable. You've made the commitment; now forge ahead.

Get out your resume. Revise or refresh it, if necessary. You may want to find a professional to help rewrite it, keeping the Internet medium in the front of your mind. Writing for the Web is more succinct. If you don't grab the attention of the reader with your first two sentences, you could be just a click away from being passed over. Think of it as online dating for jobs.

Make sure there are no typos and that your grammar is perfect. Do not lie. It will come back to bite you. When you're finished, on the left of your page, upload it into your profile. It's a good idea to print it out using the new PDF icon to the right of your picture, just to make sure everything's where it should be. Once the icon shows up, it will automatically fill in the necessary fields where you can edit as needed. When you manually fill in your past and present jobs, as well as education fields, you may want to elaborate. Know that this editing will not change the content of your PDF resume.

As you complete your profile, don't forget to do the following:

- Create a compelling headline. It's the first thing viewers see after your name.
- Perfect your summary. It's the most important part of your profile. It's your elevator pitch: You're on an elevator with someone in a corner office who asks what you do. You have 30 seconds to make a great impression. Write it down.

Complete your profile. It'll take a few hours. LinkedIn states that a completed profile makes you 40 times more likely to receive opportunities. To do that, you will need three recommendations from colleagues, classmates, and friends. Consider your well-rounded life. Are you an active school parent? Scout leader? Volunteer? All these activities can be indicators of excellent character. Use them all.

Keep your projects current and visible by utilizing the "What Are You Working on Now" field right under your headline.

There's one more critical thing to complete before you get down to the nitty-gritty job search. Prepare a basic cover letter template—one that you can tweak when necessary to tailor your pitch to a specific job description. It's your first impression. Make it count.

Now you're finally prepared to search and to apply for jobs. Click "Jobs" on the home page drop-down menu. Highlight "Find Jobs" and then type in a keyword. Don't bother with the zip code. You never know what you'll find or where. If you want part-time or freelance work, add that into the field. Pay attention to the entire left hand column. Scroll down to see many ways to refine your search.

Once you click "Apply," you'll add your cover letter. Nearly all your other information will be added automatically. While you wait for a response, keep searching.

With all the contacts you've made, someone at the job you're applying for may be one of them. And you don't need to search any further than the right side of the page.

LinkedIn gives unparalleled access to detailed information on companies throughout the world. Choose one at random, and access current and past employees, recent hires, possible contacts, and recruiters. You may e-mail any one of them, ask questions, and, again, make new contacts.

During the sign-up process, you will be asked if you'd like to upgrade your membership. This enables you to get more profile information on people outside your network, to organize profiles, and to send e-mails without introductions. Prices range from $24.95 to $499.95 per month, depending on the level. Pricey. Hold out until you're sure you need it.

The amount of information on these sites, between what you provide and what's available, is like peeling an onion. Try not to get frustrated. Work your way through it one click at a time. The results will be the success of Y.O.U., Inc.

Twitter

In addition to these and other social networking sites, don't overlook the power of Twitter. Twitter is a fantastic way for job seekers to connect with colleagues from their industries, as well as recruiters, job boards, and employers (see Appendix: Twitter Jobs and Job Sites).

Twitter enables those searching for jobs to talk directly with hiring managers—a feat simply unheard of even five years ago. Although we are not suggesting that the new hiring process entails a tweeted resume and a direct-message job offer, this platform does enable candidates with the unique opportunity to direct human resources professionals to their qualifications via links to their online resumes, blogs, or social network profile pages.

We had a client whose company announced it would cease operations at the end of the month, leaving him without his job as the company's finance director. He had been actively involved in the social media space, including a Twitter group, so when he got the news, he sent a tweet saying, "Just got laid off—Director of Finance looking for job in a Fortune 500 company—anyone have any leads?" and received direct messages from people who knew him and could offer some contacts. Within two weeks, he had secured another job—but this wasn't pure luck by any means. This individual had spent time in advance building trust, credibility, and relationships with his followers—and because the followers had come to know him, they wanted to help.

Recruiters are tuned into Twitter and are optimizing it to their advantage. For example, Christa Foley, recruiting manager at

Zappos.com at the time of this writing (@electra), routinely tweets advice for job seekers, but she does so with an eye toward potential Zappos job candidates.

On the job-seeker and recruiter side, Twitter clients. such as TweetMyJobs, enable users to subscribe to specific job channels and to receive updates to their mobile phones. In addition, countless Twitter accounts have been created with the express purpose of job recruitment and posting (see Appendix: Twitter Jobs).

To optimize the use of Twitter in your job search, begin by completing your profile. Be sure that your Twitter profile page is professional and contains a job pitch (place this in your Twitter bio section). Upload a professional photo for your avatar (no beach or party photos, please!—unless of course this relates to your desired profession).

You will then be ready to conduct a Twitter search (visit Search. Twitter.com). Seek out human resource professionals or recruiters within your desired company or industry, and begin to follow them. This will give you some first-hand insights into the companies you have identified as your top choices.

In addition to following, you will also want to tweet out your own content. Items to tweet about include your job search, information that demonstrates your expertise, help for fellow job seekers within your industry, retweets of articles of value to your industry, and so forth. The key is to establish yourself as an expert, just as you have done on your blog or Web page. Speaking of blogs and Web pages, be sure to tweet out updates to your blog via your Twitter feed, and include a link to your online resume on your profile page. Be sure to include links to your social network profiles, such as LinkedIn and Facebook, within your resume. Presenting your credentials via Twitter will enable recruiters or those who can connect you to corporate influencers to access your qualifications with ease.

PART II

Targeting

6

The Targeted Employer Search

ONE OF THE MOST COMMON and biggest mistakes we see with people who are laid off is that they panic and start their job searches without properly preparing. In other words, they fire before taking aim. This is one of the biggest mistakes a job seeker can make.

To avoid this rapid-fire misstep of sending a resume that wasn't thought through to a target that wasn't researched, we advise that you take a different approach—one that begins with careful planning.

We advise you to always have your resume updated, but beyond this we suggest that as soon as you get a new job, start updating your resume for the next job, and continue to modify your resume as you learn the scope and responsibilities of your new job.

All too often, before they come to us, our job-hunting clients have admitted that they came home after being fired and immediately started firing off resumes. Albeit, it is a very human reaction, but it is also a major misstep—again, unless you have an updated resume already prepared.

Once you put your resume out there, it's sometimes hard to pull it back, as human resources departments and recruiters might have downloaded it. Also, if you use other social media as we suggest you do, your message—your pitch for your services—will get passed on. Once it's viral, it's out of your control.

If your message goes viral, and it's the right one, that's great. If your message doesn't position you appropriately, it's not only a waste of time and may potentially lead you to missed opportunities, but it also can do damage to your online reputation. We discuss this in detail.

So the bottom line is: Don't send out your resume until you've had time to consider what you want it to do for you and where you'd like to be.

You as Broadcaster

As you begin your job search, it may help you to think of your activities as falling into one of two buckets: content or distribution.

Think of what television or radio news stations do. They gather, organize, and prepare their news stories (the messages), and then they blast them out to the world over the airwaves (distribution).

You are about to do the exact same thing, except you're going to leverage the distributive power of the Internet, and you are going to focus your message toward a particular objective—at least to some degree.

Instead of the term *broadcaster*, you may be better described as a *narrowcaster*—someone focusing a message to a targeted audience.

Of course, you'll want to spread the message that you are looking for a job as far and wide as possible. But there are only so many hours in the day, so you will want to target your efforts toward the best opportunities. We'll walk you through how to do that targeting so that you maximize your odds of getting the type of job you're looking for as efficiently as possible.

But for now, keep in mind that it's a two-step process: You're going to craft your message, and then you're going to distribute that message.

Research *before* Reaching Out

All marketers *say* that they are "customer-centric"—meaning that they strive to meet the needs of their potential and current customers. But many businesses fail, because they lose touch with their customers' needs. Instead of finding out what customers want and producing that for them, marketers sometimes blindly create products that they THINK their customers need. And then when no one buys their products, they're baffled.

Smart companies are always doing market research. And that's what you need to do, too.

The message from recruiters and senior-level executives is that you have to keep retooling and gaining new skills in this economy in order to be marketable. But the question you must ask is, "What skills do I need to get that next job?"

The answer to that question is easily available to you. If you want to find out what skills are in demand, just look at the advertisements online for jobs. You'll begin to spot patterns that you'll want to zero in on.

Doing such research will help keep you up to date with the skills you need. If you see that there is an increased demand for a certain skill set, take a class or research that topic online. You may already have that skill, but you may not be positioning yourself so that it is obvious to a recruiter or a human resources department that you have the necessary qualifications. This is why it's vital to learn the skills vocabulary from your initial research.

If you see that employers are looking for proficiency in "auto repair," and you keep seeing those keywords over and over again in job ads, then make sure your resume uses those keywords, assuming you have that skill set. Now you might also want to use the words "car maintenance" or other variations, in case those words are used as well. But the point is that you need to give the human resources department want it wants. Think of this as writing an ad for yourself and your skills that mirrors the way an employer writes a job description to attract candidates.

So when preparing to craft your message in the form of a resume and social network profile, first be sure to spend a significant amount of time reading the job sites and jotting down lists of keywords of skill sets, qualifications, and other phrases that you see your target audience using to find people with your set of skills.

How HR Looks for Candidates

We've all heard the disheartening statistic that employers look at your resume for only about five seconds before determining whether they should read more or throw it away.

But even that estimate is generous.

Faced with an almost endless sea of resumes, HR executives are busier than ever. They get flooded with resumes daily. And so what they must do is scan for keywords. They may be physically scanning resumes, but, more likely than not, they are using the services of job boards, such as Monster.com, HotJobs.com, and so forth, and searching for candidates via keywords.

This is where your keyword research comes into play.

Reverse-Engineering Your Resume

By researching ads for the types of jobs you're looking for, and pulling out keywords, you are increasing your chances of coming up in a search done by an employer.

Once you have a list of those keywords, you're going to weave them into your resume. You may even have a section in your resume—called "Skills" perhaps—where you simply list your skills one after another. In digital marketing, this is called "keyword packing".

But don't just rely on what you see on online job boards. When you do get an interview, ask recruiters and human resources executives how they found you. If they say that they did a search, ask them about what keywords they used.

Remember, your research should not extend only as far as your next job. You'll want to do ongoing research because the job market is changing rapidly—and so, too, are the buzzwords that people use to describe in-demand skills.

Crafting Your Message: It's Not about You

Even though in this section, we talk about how to position YOURSELF and how to prepare YOUR message, keep one thing in mind: It's not about YOU! It's about THEM: your prospective, future employers. In marketing, the acronym for this concept is WIIFM, which stands for What's in It for Me?

The ME in this case is the employer—the consumer, the buyer, the potential purchaser of the product called YOU. So when preparing your commercial, think of your audience, and approach it from the perspective of how you can help it further ITS goals. Ask yourself such questions as:

- How can I generate more revenue for its company?
- How can I cut costs?
- How can I make its company more efficient?
- How can I help the specific person who is going to hire me?

Benefits versus Features

Another key concept in product marketing (and make no mistake, at this stage, you are packaging yourself as a product) is the distinction between product features and product benefits.

Features are you-focused. They tell about who you are.

Here are some features that you might be including in your resume:

1. Where you live
2. Where you went to school
3. Your activities in the community
4. Your hobbies

As we discuss, there may be some advantage to sharing at least some of these personal aspects of yourself. However, we'd like you to err on the side of focusing on benefits.

The Power of Benefits

Just as features are *you*-focused, benefits are *them*-focused. It gets back to WIIFM— again, where the ME is the prospective employer.

What are you offering? How can your employer use your skills to further its ends?

Some examples of benefits are:

1. Your specific skills

Not just a list of them, but rather how they can be applied to the needs of your prospective employer. Don't assume that the recruiters see the connection. You have to connect the dots and paint the picture for them. We show you exactly how to do this.

2. Your specific accomplishments in past jobs

Even though we want you to use specifics—for reasons of credibility—you also must keep in mind that you want to make it clear how your past accomplishments can translate into concrete results for your prospective employer.

When we do online marketing consulting, our tagline is: "More Clicks. More Cash. We focus on results." Of course, that's just a tagline to grab attention, but we can back that up with case studies and specific numbers showing how we increased traffic to our clients' sites and then increased sales.

You have to do the same—get attention by talking about how you can get results.

Remember, WIIFM. All job search applicants fall into the trap of focusing on themselves—even us. From when we are children all the way through our adult lives, we're asked to stand up and tell about ourselves. And most of those mini speeches are focused on features. We're here to break you of this habit.

Yes, of course, there has to be something in it for you—a meaningful job, a decent wage, benefits, an acceptable work environment, potential for growth. But mostly, you're one of a steady stream of people who would love to have the job that you are seeking.

We're not saying that you are not special. We're not saying that you are a commodity. But be aware that there are droves of competitors out there, and it's your job to separate yourself from the pack. In marketing terms, this is known as differentiating yourself.

This perspective is especially important when the demand for jobs outstrips supply. When there are many jobs available, and therefore numerous options for you as a job hunter, you can afford to be picky. But you might be in a position right now in which you need to be somewhat less selective—again, at least for now—if only to pay the rent.

People Seek Out Sameness

Humans are social beings. From our earliest beginnings, we formed clans to share in common defense against predators or to use the power of numbers to hunt and to gather food. We shared the work and the rewards.

Even before the advent of social technologies, people searched for connections with others. We tend to befriend people who are like us. We connect more readily with those who share the same worldview or hobbies or interests.

Social networks simply speed up the meeting-and-greeting process by providing technologies that allow you to search for those whom you may know from your past or those who have common interests. At least some amount of face-to-face networking has been replaced by online networking.

But it's still all about making the social connection.

So keep in mind that even though we say that you need to focus mostly on benefits, features also should be included. Features may form a basis for those crucial connections, and the right features often give hiring companies clues about how well you may perform for them.

If you've invested a significant amount of time, money, and effort in education, that's usually a fairly good indication that you are a hard worker. Your interests or community-service involvement may give a new connection some idea of your values and priorities. Are you an intellectually curious person? Are you doing your part to making the world a better place? These traits are noticed.

As far as making connections, you may have more luck finding a job through alumni of the trade school, college, or university you attended, because you will find an instant, natural connection.

Those who do the hiring in companies will often admit that they hired someone because they liked and trusted that person due to some personal connection, no matter how small. Product marketers spend billions each year trying to convince consumers that the people who use their products are like them. They try to build empathy and trust with their target audiences, as they know that this will increase the likelihood that someone will buy.

As we've noted earlier, this means that you don't want to be strictly business. You want to include at least some personal information. It is your decision as to what you want to divulge, yet the more you share, the more people will typically disclose to you. That personal connection may very well give you the edge in your job hunt.

The Need for Versions

In Chapter 4, we explain the concept of versioning. Before we get into how to write your benefit-packed personal commercial, we want you to keep in mind that it is most effective if you can vary how you position yourself to different employers.

To be clear: Do not pretend to be something you aren't. In fact, your positioning may require only slight tweaks, depending on the range of jobs or fields that you're targeting. However, being flexible in how you can present yourself can give you an edge by expanding the pool of employers who might be interested in hiring you.

You can do this by preparing multiple versions of how you present yourself both orally and in writing to a variety of employers. We gave an example earlier about how to do this on a resume. For example, a software developer could have one resume that focuses on coding experience but another that emphasizes awareness of the management side of the software development lifecycle. The two versions could tee him up to pursue jobs as either an individual contributor or as a manager of other technically inclined employees.

Likewise, this individual needs to be prepared to use a versioning philosophy when interviewing as well. Thus, our software developer should prepare some benefit-packed personal commercials that highlight specific instances in which he proved to be a superstar coder while also readying some stories that will position him as a collaborative team member and leader on software projects.

Social networking technologies will expand your ability to reach people with your message, but differentiating your positioning even slightly will expand your potential audience even more.

Writing Benefit Statements with the PAR Formula

Earlier, we briefly allude to the PAR Formula. Let's delve more deeply into this concept here. If you observe effective television ads, you'll start noticing a simple pattern. You can't get too complex in 30 seconds. First, there's not much time to pitch a product. Second, the audience doesn't pay too much attention to ads, as it has learned to tune them out due to information overload.

We all know all too well that we are bombarded by messages trying to sell us something every day, whether it is through TV, radio, blinking ads on the Internet, billboards, or telemarketers interrupting our dinners.

Just as advertisers have to cut through the clutter and make enough of an impact to at least get your attention, you also must find a way to stand out from the pile of resumes that are sitting on top of—and underneath—yours on the desk of the person who may hire you.

That's where the PAR formula comes in. As we note briefly earlier, PAR stands for Problem, Action, Result. Let's walk through the specifics of the formula and how its application can help you in your job search.

Problem

Think of a commercial for a weight-loss product.

First, it will hit you with the common problem. It may ask a question: "Are you overweight? Do you have less energy?" This sort of query may be accompanied by images of overweight people suffering from the symptoms of their unwanted condition. The advertiser is reaching out to its potential audience, trying to identify with and to empathize with those who are struggling with the problem and who therefore might be potential consumers of its product.

That's the Problem Step.

Action

Next comes the Action Step, which provides the answer to the problem at hand.

What is the answer to all your problems as laid out in the Problem Step? The advertiser's product, naturally.

So it's the job of the Problem Step to get the attention of qualified buyers. It must get individuals in the audience to say, "Yes, that's me!" and then remind them of the pain that the problem is causing them.

The Action Step is a quick one. In so many words, it's simply, "Buy our product or service."

And then finally, the advertiser is going to tell you why its product is the solution.

Results

How do marketers attempt to make this answer to the problem plausible? They will attempt to show that their products get results.

The benefits of the products are then presented.

"If you buy our product, then you'll experience X, Y, and Z results, and the problem will be solved for you."

How PAR Relates to the Product of YOU

Just as the weight-loss product marketer is looking for a relevant audience that might buy its product and then try to get the members' attention, you are engaged in the same process when it comes to job hunting.

The problem that you say you can solve has to be general enough to capture a fairly broad group of potential employers. That's not that hard to do. As we mention above, you're going to help by either increasing a company's revenues, decreasing its costs by making it more efficient, or perhaps supporting others in the organization who affect the bottom line more directly.

The key is that you want to be specific when it comes to results.

When thinking through the problems you can solve, reflect upon what results you have accomplished. Be sure to focus on successes that you've had that can be beneficial to your potential employer.

Focusing on problem solving will help you position your skills as transferable. In other words, your skills will be just as relevant to future employers as they were to your past employers.

Examples of PAR

The following are examples of PAR formulas that you may use to spark your thinking about how to position yourself:

A Revenue Generator: Marketing

> *Problem*: I have worked with companies in the software industry that have been struggling to keep up with growing competition and the rising costs of advertising.

> *Action*: I've planned and executed integrated marketing plans that hatve enabled my past employers to do more with fewer marketing dollars. I oversaw adding new marketing channels, including new cable television ads

as well as a variety of Internet marketing campaigns, by leveraging advertising programs from Google, Yahoo!, and MSN.

Results: Due to my team's efforts, traffic to our Web site has increased by 27 percent from X to Y unique visitors over the last six months. Overall revenue from all marketing channels has increased by 36 percent to a total of $2.6 million, and our cost per customer acquisition has dropped by 14 percent.

An Efficiency Expert: Accounting

Problem: I have worked for companies in X, Y, and Z industries that were struggling with merging and stream-lining their accounting systems. I have led major financial analysis and budgeting projects for financially troubled companies that quickly had to go through turnarounds.

Action: I used my financial analysis skills and experience working in a wide variety of industries to enable senior managers to get a better sense of expenses across departments that in turn helped them get costs under control. I've also implemented new accounting policies and procedures that have ensured that the companies were in compliance with all relevant accounting standards.

Results: As a result of the several financial analysis projects that I managed, we were able to cut overall expenses by 18 percent as well as reduce financial and accounting staff in the process. Before I took my most recent position, the company often was found to not be in compliance, and the accounting department had to work significant overtime to rectify problems discovered by our external auditors. During my tenure, we have been in full compliance, which, in combination with efficiency efforts, contributed to the significant cost reductions mentioned earlier.

Remember that your PARs are works in progress. They are always evolving as you do market research as to what gets people's attention and what helps you land more interviews.

You will always want to be testing. Try new angles on presenting yourself to see if you are more comfortable in positioning your accomplishments differently, and, again, test-drive different Ps, As, and Rs to see what works best.

In any case, be ready to modify your PARs to key off what your interviewer asks you.

The Medium and the Message

Even though we focus later on how to get your message out there through different methods of distribution, we strongly suggest that you spend a significant amount of time doing the market research and crafting your message as described above.

Again, it's no use putting time, effort, and money into spreading your message if it's not an effective one that will result in job leads.

When crafting your PARs, we suggest that you write several of them down in many drafts and many versions. With each PAR, err on the side of writing more at first and then editing down. By brainstorming first and thinking outside the proverbial box, you may stumble upon an angle that differentiates you from the rest of the pack.

However, keep in mind that even though you are writing down the message, you will be broadcasting—or, as we said, narrowcasting—it in many forms. You will be using it to:

- Write your resumes
- Write your cover letters
- Update your social networking profiles
- Prepare orally for your interviews
- Perhaps put together a video presentation of your skills

You are going to write it, but then you will use it over and over again. And you'll keep modifying it over and over again. Think of this as an exercise in writing poetry—succinct, to-the-point, high-impact communication—where every word in your brand message counts.

Owning Your Search Engine Results Page

Now that you have an understanding of how to develop your message, let's go into greater detail on how to transmit it via the Internet. Back in Chapter 3, we talk about snapping up a Web domain that includes some form of your name. But even if you own such a URL, there's no guarantee it will come up as the first entry in the search engine results page (SERP) when someone does a search for you.

Search engines don't only look at the Web address when serving up relevant results to any given search. There are many factors that go into any search engine's algorithm, the behind-the-scenes equation that determines which results are presented to the search engine user. So how do you make sure that you show up at the top of the search results?

First of all, your goal should be to DOMINATE the SERP that is served up when someone does a search on your name. You do that by creating and controlling the content that is written or posted about you—if we're talking photos or video.

Creating SPC: Self-Promotional Content

Self-Promotional Content (SPC) does not refer to content that you designed to sing your own praises. Rather, this is content that professionally positions you as an expert in your field.

In the past, if you wanted to be the expert, you had to write a book. You can still write a book, and it's easier and cheaper than ever. But even faster and easier is to simply start writing on a topic you know well that relates to your job search.

Writing Articles

If you don't have the time or inclination to write consistently on a topic, simply start with an article, even if it's just a summary of current issues, problems, and solutions in your area of expertise.

Once you have written articles or blog posts, you want to leverage that content. That is, you want to get it in as many places as possible. You want to maximize distribution so as to maximize the exposure you get as an expert. You never know who might read an article and contact you for consulting, a part-time job, or even full-time employment.

So after you have written, edited, and polished your content, submit it to article submission sites, such as www.ideamarketers.com, www.ezinearticles.com, or www.articlesbase.com. And if you get into it and start writing more articles, it might be a first step to blogging—or maybe even putting together a whole book on a topic.

Using Squidoo

Beyond the article sites above, check out Squidoo.com. Squidoo is a site that enables you to easily set up—for free—a page on a topic of your choice—whether it is of personal interest or professional expertise.

The site is a collection of linked, user-generated "lenses," which are nothing more than individual pages, each on a specific topic. You can create as many lenses as you want to highlight your perspective, recommendations, and/or expertise.

You can even use Squidoo by carving up your book into paragraphs that focus on themes and posting them in different lenses. The more articles you have out there, the greater the opportunity you have to be found.

There are thousands of articles on various topics. As we show in the next section, you may want to research and to link to articles related to your area of expertise. Squidoo could be a good hunting ground for high-quality articles.

Many people link to Squidoo, so articles on the site generally rank high in related SERPs. Make sure you include your name and contact information in the entry so that the articles are related to you when picked up by the search engines.

Squidoo is also recommended because Google finds and displays lens pages quickly, because the site is constantly updated by many people. Google sees it as a site with large amounts of expert content, constantly being refreshed and thus more relevant than more static sites.

As a contributor to Squidoo, you also get to share in the advertising revenue of the site. At the time of this writing, you as a content contributor get 50 percent of the ad revenue associated with your content. You're probably not going to get rich off of creating Squidoo lenses, but it is a nice extra benefit.

The Keys to Getting Good Visibility with Squidoo

The main key to getting exposure through Squidoo is keywords. Make sure to use common keywords that are related to your subject-matter expertise. Again, that's why you started with market research.

So don't skip that first step. If you're going to take the time and effort to write articles, you want them to get maximum exposure, so find out what the popular keywords in your field are.

Squidoo is great, because it encourages you to promote your personal agenda, expertise, causes, products, and opinions. As we suggest above, though, focus on educating rather than advertising. Remember, you're trying to show those who might hire you that you can add value for their benefit. Be customer-centric. As you post lenses, think of how you can help your audience of those who are looking for advice on your topic.

Make sure you include your bio and links to your blog, site, and other articles or lenses you might have written.

Finally, as with regular social networks, Squidoo has groups—minicommunities of people who are interested in similar topics. You should join relevant groups and subtly promote yourself as an expert in those groups.

Gathering OPAs—Other People's Articles

If you look at most blogs, you'll see that one of their columns might have a list of links to related articles, whether written by the blogger or by others.

This is typically called a blogroll. Even if you just write a couple of blog posts, you might want to have a blogroll. This simple list will show that you keep up with articles that are relevant to your subject area.

This can be very helpful to someone reading your blog. And if that person can refer you to someone else for a job, it may impress him or her enough to contact you or even to hire you.

Blogging

Many people have personal blogs where they comment and post photos or videos about their hobbies or pets or children. We don't want to dissuade you from doing that, but realize that *any* content about you is out there. If it conflicts with your professional goals, you may want to rethink your strategy.

If you are serious about positioning yourself as an expert on the Internet, you might consider putting such personal content in a private blog where people can only access the content with your permission. Or perhaps you might want to put it in a private section on your social network. More on that later.

If you blog, write short articles, or even just pull together links to articles, you'll not only have a better shot at crowding out the competition by ranking high on the SERP, you'll also show a potential employer that you are actively researching and participating in your area of expertise. That will only increase your credibility.

In this competitive job market, a topical and well-written blog can be enough of a differentiator to lead an employer to hire one candidate over another. If you don't have the time or inclination to write consistently on a topic, simply start with an article. It doesn't have to feature a revolutionary idea. It might just be a summary of current issues, problems, and solutions in your area of expertise. Once you have written, edited, and proofread this piece, submit it to sites that accept articles from outside commentators.

Choose a Niche

First, you have to pick an area of expertise that you want to write about. You don't want to pick something too narrow—or something too broad.

Let the market research that we discuss above guide you. What subject areas are employers looking for right now? Maybe focusing on cost-cutting measures is advisable, especially if this is an area in which you excel. If you're a marketing guru, perhaps buzz marketing or niche marketing would be a cool concept. The possibilities are endless. Pick an area that you can write about passionately and that will showcase you as a content expert.

Select a Blogging Platform

There are many different solutions out there that will get you up and blogging quickly. Some of the most popular blogging software solutions include Wordpress.com, Blogger.com, and TypePad.com. If you know a little bit of programming, you can even use these platforms to create an entire Web site.

If you want to create a site that looks more like a traditional Web site as opposed to a blog, and if you don't want to waste time learning how to design and to code, check out the inexpensive, easy-to-use software solution at www.SiteBuildIt.com, which we highly recommend.

Design Your Blog

All blog platforms provide you with basic designs, but if you want to get fancy—and you know how to do a bit of coding or can afford to hire someone who does—you might want to make your site look a bit more professional. There are prefabricated site designs available through sites such as www.TemplateMonster.com.

If you want to get your hands dirty, you can dig into the HTML code of the blog's basic template and use cascading style sheets (CSS), which is a coding language used to add style—fonts, colors, spacing, layout—to Web pages.

If you want to learn the basics of HTML and CSS, check out the free tutorials on www.W3Schools.com. HTML is surprisingly easy to learn, and knowledge of it can prove handy in a variety of fields.

But again, this is totally optional, as a clean, simple template provided by the blog platforms listed above is usually good enough. Unless you are a Web designer trying to get clients, a simple page with your bio information on it is usually sufficient.

Producing Podcasts

If you're not a writer, you can create a podcast on your area of expertise. A podcast is simply an audio recording that is available in a digital file that can be uploaded to the Web.

Not everyone is a reader, so you want to make sure that your content is available to those who would rather listen to your expertise. People can download your podcasts, store them on their iPods or other audio players, and listen to them on the go.

There is plenty of recording equipment out there that is inexpensive and easy to use. You can even record directly onto your computer. Here are a few suggestions on recording equipment:

- You can record your podcasts by using a Lavelier microphone, which will give you fairly good sound quality. You want the podcast to sound as if it were recorded professionally.
- The digital recorder we use is a Marantz Professional PMD620, but, again, there are many that you can use. Just search for digital recorders on Amazon.com, find some in your price range, and read the reviews.

Podcast Distribution

You will want to give your podcasts the widest distribution possible. The more people who hear you talk about your expertise, the better your chances of getting job leads.

So make them available on your site. They are simply files that you can upload and make available for download. Check the instructions for how to do so within the help sections of the blog software that you choose.

Also, submit your podcasts to Apple's iTunes. Whether you distribute them on your blog, site, or iTunes, you can either give your podcasts away for free or charge for them. Given that you are looking for broad distribution and your goal is to promote yourself as an expert, we recommend giving away your podcasts.

So if you are more of a talker than a writer, explore podcasting.

Your Social Network Profiles

Once you have crafted your message, your PARs, and some self-promotional content, it's time to put it on display on social networks so that you can reach the maximum number of people possible.

Social Networks

There are literally hundreds if not thousands of social networks. You can start one of your own within minutes by using such services as Ning or KickApps, which are known as private-label social media platforms. Fees vary across these platforms (many are free or come with a nominal monthly fee).

Just because there are many social networks doesn't mean that you should spend your time posting a profile on all of them. We recommend you pick five or six and focus your energies in monitoring and testing them.

Given their popularity, we suggest you post profiles on Facebook, LinkedIn, and MySpace—in that order. Facebook is wildly popular. LinkedIn is seen as a professional social-networking site, and MySpace is popular as well despite its reputation for being less professional and more for kids and music bands. But that doesn't mean you shouldn't test it as a hunting ground for jobs. It is important to direct prospective employers to a controlled environment. As you now know, human resource executives, recruiters, and hiring managers will look for information about you online to check you out before they even invite you in to speak to them.

They don't want to waste their precious time. They want to weed out anyone who doesn't meet their hiring criteria. The same goes for people who will refer you on to others.

They want to be known for having recommended quality people so that they look good when they recommend you for a job and you turn out to be a good fit. They want to be seen in a good light by recruiters and human resource executives so that when it's their turn to look for a job, their networks will remember them as having done them good favors.

Links to Your Content

After you spend the time creating your self-promotional content, make sure people can easily find it.

Include links in such places as your e-mail signature file, which is at the bottom of every one of your e-mails that you send out related to your job search. Also include them on both your paper and electronic resumes and at the end of messages that you send through social network message systems.

You will want to provide links to your online resume, your online bio, your posted articles, your social network profiles, your podcasts, and your videos. You might not want to overdo it, so you may want to have a short list of links to content that presents you in the most positive or relevant light. But err on the side of the more, the merrier.

If you do manage to get people's attention, you want to increase your chances of keeping their attention and getting them to take action. Provide access to all your SPC. If someone doesn't want to be bothered reading it, so be it. But if he or she wants to check it out, it's right there.

Become a Job Magnet

One of the most frustrating parts of looking for a job is that you have to get other people to at least give you a chance to show them what you've got. Getting in the door is the hardest part.

But when you become an expert, others seek you out. Or, at least, when you knock on the door, at least some people will hear you out for a bit longer if they think you know something that could help them.

You want to be like a magnet—pulling people toward you— instead of having to push yourself on others. By creating good-quality Self-Promotional Content, you'll prove that you are a problem solver. You'll show that you can add value, and therefore others who need what you have to offer will contact you.

So, again, before you say to yourself that you aren't going to put the work into creating content that promotes your expertise, realize that your competition is doing it. In the past, being perceived as an expert was a nice-to-have asset. Today, it's a need-to-have element.

Target Your Employer Wish List

Again, remember that your paper resume, social network profile, and social media resume are the message. They are your advertise-ment, a commercial of you.

But before you craft and fine-tune that message to take advantage of leveraging online social networking and social media channels, you need to know who your audience is. Why? Because it will affect how you present—or, as it is known in marketing, "position"—yourself. So, beginning with the end in mind, and with some direction, ask yourself, "Where do I want to work?"

As you proceed in both your people and company search, you'll come up with new ideas for places you want to work, or you may find that you can't break in to your original targets, so you might modify your targets.

Examples of a "top X" employer wish list could be the direct competitors to your prior or current firm. However, if you have signed a noncompete agreement, that could get sticky.

Note that, although meant to protect a company from customer defections or loss of proprietary intellectual property, at their core, these agreements can be challengeable in court depending on legal precedents and the particular states in which the agreements were executed. But no company can legally prohibit you from earning a living. If they choose, big companies with dedicated legal departments and deep pockets can make your life hell should you choose to test the agreement that you have signed.

JOB SEEKER SUCCESS STORY:
Follow That Recruiter!

Doug Hamlin, a 23-year-old Web developer, obtained a new job just by keeping tabs on his industry.

Hamlin responded to an appeal by the Minneapolis firm Weber Shandwick looking for an information technology professional. The firm's digital strategy manager, Greg Swan, posted the opening for an HTML language developer to his Twitter account's 2,000 followers. The simple post used 136 of the 140-character limit and was enough to get Hamlin to respond with his resume and information.

Using the network to follow recruiters is a good way to quickly find opportunities to expand a career or to find a new job, according to professional recruiter Shane Bernstein, who runs an IT talent agency in Los Angeles, California.

"Social networks are going to take over job boards," Bernstein says, adding that connections with others in professional fields through these networks make it easier to approach someone making hiring decisions.

In addition to following recruiters for various companies, users can also become fans of different enterprises on Facebook. Firms may use these pages to announce job openings before they are published on job boards or in the more traditional medium of classified advertisements.

Getting your resume in among the first group of applicants, like Hamlin did, can help you stand out from other candidates and could also help you get a job faster. Knowing what jobs in the industry are opening up as soon as possible can also help you get a good idea of what the market is like in the industry.

SOURCE: Dickler, Jessica. "I Found My Job on Twitter." CNN/Money.com, 12 May 2009 <http://money.cnn.com/2009/05/12/news/economy/social_networking_jobs/index.htm >.

Other examples of a top-employer wish list could be key suppliers or vendors to your past or current company or select distributors/ dealers in your firms' sales distribution channel.

So as a reminder, the first step is to write down a list of the top 10 companies you'd like to work for. Of course, there is no magic in the number 10—you might have a top 20—but we want you to start with a limited set of targets, ideally, no more than two dozen. Why start this way?

This targeted "short list" is important, because it acts as a jumping-off point to your main personal network contacts—those most closely known by you.

You will be communicating this target list to them. If you list too many, you can end up causing confusion and dilute the effectiveness of those who may be able to help you.

Specific Industries and Types of Companies

Second, beyond writing down your wish list of specific companies, you will also want to think of three or four different *types* of companies that you are looking to target.

Take your wish list of specific companies, and think of the types of companies that they represent. Also think about grouping them by industry, and then make a list of those firms, too.

Here's an example: Let's say you worked for, or are currently with, Dell Computer. You've already made a list of Dell's competitors (HP, IBM, Toshiba, etc.) as part of your wish list.

- Been a PC lover? How about considering switching horses to Apple and key MAC product vendors? There's a whole new universe of potential employers there you might never have thought of. *Make a list.*
- What about chip/semiconductor manufacturers, such as Intel and AMD? *Make another list.*
- How about monitor manufacturers, such as Nokia, Samsung, and the like? *Make a third list.*
- Or perhaps look at a different angle, and go behind the scenes to computer OEMs who sell to the Dells of the world. They make key parts, such as motherboards, soundcards, graphic cards, and SCSI cards. *Keep going!* Brainstorm, and let your mind run wild.

That's the kind of "lateral thinking" we are suggesting. Don't filter, and be open to anything, because you never know where the next opportunity will come from. It might very well be one you never heard or thought of before.

Don't get too broad. Lack of focus in communicating your target industry of interest to others (e.g., health-care industry) will get you very little help, because it's too vague.

To maximize the help your personal network can provide in your company/people search, your contacts need specific direction. A list of targeted firms does just that. You'll want to narrow that down and say, for example, that you are looking for a position in a company that deals in health-care medical recordkeeping.

This is not to discourage you from thinking broadly but rather to encourage you to avoid scattering your energies in too many directions.

Research Data Sources

When conducting market research on potential employer companies, you may find you need a starting point. Some resource directories, some free and some subscription-based, include:

- Standard and Poor's Directory
  This is a solid source of companies, searchable by SIC/ NAIC industry codes. The company info is generally brief, and you will only find the contact names/titles of upper management.
- Dun and Bradstreet Directory
- Thomas' Industrial Directory
  This directory has a commercial / industrial company focus with limited info.
- Ward's Business Directory

This one has straightforward data with more detailed industry and company information than offered in the S&P and D&B directories.

- CorpTech Directory
  This is a unique directory with a high-tech industry focus on 17 major markets. It includes many hard-to-find, privately held companies. It's a great resource.

Online Business Directory Resources (Subscription-Based)

- www.Hoovers.com
- www.OneSource.com

Other Online Resources

The following resource links offer a broad range of listings of a variety of directory resources. Access is mostly free. As with any research, it takes time to wade through and find ones that can provide you the specific information and value that you seek, but patience and perseverance can really pay off here.

- www.Business.com/
- www.Google.com/Top/Business/Directories/
- https://dir.yahoo.com/Business_and_Economy/ Directories/
- www.IPL.org/div/subject/browse/bus15.00.00/

In addition to the above-mentioned resources, there are numerous other directories and online databases, many specific to a particular industry or market.

It can be a daunting and frustrating task if you've never had exposure to or spent much time doing this sort of research, but don't feel discouraged. Invest some time, and visit your main public library. Due to the subscription costs of many directories, library branches often have very few or none of the main resources, which are typically held at the main branches and not loaned out.

Introduce yourself to the business section librarian. Explain that you are doing a job search and want to research companies and company information and that you could use some help. He or she will be happy to help point you to the resources both in the stacks and in online databases that can help you. If you're not finding what you need, ask for more assistance.

7

The Targeted People Search

Who's in Your Circle

EACH OF US HAS A CIRCLE of friends, acquaintances, colleagues, co-workers, parents from the PTA, fellow soccer coaches, members of the knitting club, and so forth. Many job seekers have robust circles of connections in the offline realm. In the online space, the circles can vary somewhat dramatically. In the online environment, ask yourself, "Whom am I connected to?" and "Through which social networking sites am I connected to them?"

For those of you who are already using social networking aggressively for people searching and professional career-oriented networking, you have already established a great foundation—well done! If you are not quite as social networking/social media savvy or up to speed as you may be on the "people/career search" curve, now is the time to start.

Even if you have been a longtime social network user for personal connections, you may not be aware of how best to employ social networking as a central part of your career-building activities or on behalf of people searching as a tool to drive job leads.

Most people are still using online social communities as they were originally intended. They use them as "social communication/stay in touch/what's up" vehicles with their "connections" tending to be more of the friends and family variety as opposed to business/professional networking contacts.

Personal Networks and Circles of Influence

The term *circles of influence* is one more familiar to those of us in sales/business development roles (particularly those in the insurance business) and those with a strong background in professional networking. It's not a term that means much to those outside these areas.

It refers to an individual's personal contacts, specifically those who exert some level of influence on others around them—their "circle."

The influence or "sway" that they have may be due to several factors: their standing in the community or business world, special educational achievements, unique/special talents/skills, dynamic/magnetic personality, high moral/ethical character, polished speaking skills, or military prowess. Because of these traits, these individuals are looked up to and command a level of respect and credibility that others may not possess, and they tend to be well connected to other important people.

And as a result of their influence, these centers of influence can be very helpful in opening doors for others, whether to new business opportunities/deals, access to VIPs or "inside" political contacts/powerful people, and important financial/banking connections. However, this ONLY applies if you know them and they know you. Remember that *relationship building/social networking is a two-way street.*

And when it comes to career/job help, having several of these folks whom you know and are known to you on some personal level can be worth its weight in gold.

They can point you toward others you don't yet know who may be able to help you with your people search. Remember, always focus on people/relationships first; job opportunities follow.

Certainly, you have a competitive advantage if you have several solid centers of influence in your personal network of family, friends, and business acquaintances. You can always tap them if you need help of some sort that they can provide.

By starting with the people you know personally, connecting in an ever-widening network to others they know, and continuing to connect to additional contacts, you will come across and develop NEW centers of influence.

It's those folks and your proper approach and cultivation that can and will result in helping you tap into others that they know. They will aid in your people-search process and ultimate goal of realizing a satisfactory employment opportunity and perhaps many more.

JOB SEEKER SUCCESS STORY:
"I Worked at Yahoo! Until Today"

Ryan Kuder was just one of hundreds laid off from Yahoo! in 2008. The San Jose, California, resident quickly used the immediacy of Twitter to give followers a minute-by-minute accounting of his unemployment struggle.

Twitter allows members to update followers of their activities in real time by using a brief summary of only 140 characters. The followers can get the updates by visiting the site or have the updates forwarded to their mobile devices, such as cell phones or BlackBerrys.

Besides keeping his "tweeps" (people following his Twitter status updates) abreast of his job search, Kuder also set up a special group on Facebook for ex-Yahoo! workers called "I worked at Yahoo! until today" to let others know they were not alone in their plight.

In just two days, a Microsoft executive contacted Kuder about an opportunity at that company. Kuder did not join Microsoft but eventually started his own Internet company partnership with one of his Twitter followers during his unemployed days. His search also became the subject of several news stories in the local media at the time.

Kuder is just one of a growing number of people who said they used these social networking sites to either obtain employment or to get work for their existing businesses, ranging from real estate and insurance to music and the arts.

Facebook has an application available with CareerBuilder.com to help job seekers that are already on the service. This application and a couple similar ones boast some 26,000 members.

SOURCE: Rosenbloom, Stephanie. "Looking for Work on Facebook." *New York Times,* 1 May 2008 <http://www.nytimes.com/2008/05/01/fashion/01networking.html>.

Power Referrals…Plug into the Juice

Referrals are the name of the game. And more to the point are power referrals. These can include centers of influence, but your referrals certainly don't have to be. Your referrals can turn on some serious social networking "juice" for you.

In social networking lingo, a power referral is someone you may know—or if you don't, you can gain an introduction to—who can help get you introduced to other people they know whom you want or need to reach, such as a hiring authority at one of your Top 10 companies.

In some cases, these power referrers can open the door to *multiple* people you want to talk to. The best-case scenario is that you develop a really good relationship with them, resulting in their becoming your advocates and/or coaches. This makes them extremely valuable to your people-search cause and ultimate objective.

Power referrers can be immensely helpful, but they need to be nurtured and developed before you can approach them with your main goals. This may mean getting introduced to them and having them get you an introduction to the people they know. From the first contact/introduction through building your relationship, how you approach them is a key to moving your agenda forward.

Start with Your Core Personal Network

It doesn't matter if you have 5, 50, or 500 people you know in your current personal network. This is your core: Start with them. Even though these are people you know personally—friends, acquaintances, relatives, business peers, co-workers, church contacts—you still want to start your approach with the social side of things.

The first thing is ensure your list is as complete as possible. Why? Because every single one of those people knows someone else. Maybe it's just seven, but maybe it's several thousand other people. You don't know. Nor do you know where your next career opportunity will come from. Life is strange that way. Never overlook anyone. Leave no stone unturned.

You will want to divide your core list into two groups—those who you know well and with whom you're in contact regularly and those who don't know you nearly as well (but need to).

If you have a strong existing relationship and regular communication with a contact, you can jump right in, broadcasting your message of a needed job change or new employment. Hopefully that will produce some potential employer "interest" or news of job openings to pursue.

The other part of your list—those family, more casual friends, and acquaintances who don't really know you that well or with whom you're not in touch regularly—will require more effort, as you will need to start forging closer connections with them.

Because there's some sort of prior connection in place already, reach out to them, but not about your job situation. Start with a "Hi, what's new, how've you been?" approach.

Reestablish the rapport or connection you initially made. Find or rediscover common ground and interests. Learn what's new with the family, their life, their kids, vacations they've taken, recent home improvements, or mutual friends in common. Show interest—sincere and genuine interest. And actively LISTEN to what they have to say which will help you reconnect with them.

Build on your reconnecting efforts with multiple follow-ups, but do it naturally. You don't want to leave the impression with them of, "What does he or she WANT with me?"

Once you've rebuilt these relationships, *then* you can ask for some help and share your employment situation/needs. Due to having had a prior connection with them, it will take less time to get to this point than if you were starting from scratch.

Depending on how "local" your core network is, you can integrate some more traditional networking avenues into your plans. Move to arranging a lunch meeting to find out more about their jobs, industryies, and work. Ask for suggestions, help with a resume review, or general advice. It's about creating and nurturing trust, credibility, and likeability.

Set yourself a schedule of calling on and talking with a certain number of your personal network each day, week, and month. Commit to following through and doing what you set out to do. And do it consistently.

Expanding Your Core Personal Network

Okay, now here's where it starts to get interesting.

It's not who you know but who knows YOU that really counts. The more people who know YOU, the greater your exposure will be to potential career opportunities.

To frame it another way…it's NOT who's in your core personal network—IT'S WHO **THEY** KNOW. THOSE are the people you want to meet and the connections you're interested in cultivating.

You need to realize that not everyone you come across as a result of your peoples earching is going to be equally connected to others nor as valuable to you in your people search. Some folks—for different reasons—aren't deeply plugged into the social networks, while others are.

You want to look for the former group—those who are more plugged in—for they are more likely to have a larger group of social networking contacts. This can help you expand and extend your personal online social network and thus increase your exposure to new career opportunities.

So set up a minifile on each of these people in your core network who know you well, including names of their companies and any other information you discover that could be helpful down the road.

Identify and Add Value to New Influencers

Now, take your list of personal contacts, friends, or family, and pay a visit to www.LinkedIn.com. One at a time, search for their names, and, if you find them, make notes of how many other connections they have.

Then, assuming you're allowed to see your friends' connections, click through and do the same thing. Note that on LinkedIn, you can choose to have all your contacts viewable by anyone, or you can restrict that view.

If you can view the people connecting to your friends' contacts, you'll also be able to see detailed info about them, including their employers. If the firms where they work are of interest to you, add them to your potential employer list.

You can further extend your social network by doing the same thing as above, and following your contacts' contacts to *their* contacts. Now you're reaching a *third* degree of separation! You are looking for folks who have a good number of connections. As a general rule, you want to look for people on LinkedIn with at least 50 or more connections.

That's an indication, although not an absolute guarantee, that they're more tuned into social media. That may mean that they understand the concept of networking and are likely active networkers to some extent. Therefore, they can potentially be of greater help.

Although not a given, these more-connected people are also more likely than others to belong to other social networking sites, such as Twitter, Facebook, and other applications. This becomes important, because they have many more potential connections for you, and they are more tapped into what's going on in their world in terms of jobs and opportunities.

Beyond LinkedIn

As you work through this process of identifying potential influencers on LinkedIn, you can take this a step or two further.

More actively networked people may have profiles on other social networks, and they can be an additional source of new contacts for you. There is definitely overlap. Each social network has different types of people it attracts as a result of the types of interests its members have.

As an example, you will probably find some of your family's and friends' contacts on one social networking site, others who are on two sites, and yet other friends on one or two of these sites or perhaps completely different sites.

Using this approach to gather, to identify, and to expand your social network of contacts, can keep you so busy that you might not consider using other resources.

However, if you want to do an even more comprehensive job, particularly in finding other contacts working in specific companies that you are targeting, then lead generation tools can really help.

Online Lead Generation Tools

Lead generation tools/resources are more known to those of us in sales, marketing, or business development roles, as opposed to the rest of the public.

As your livelihood is dependent on your ability to find the right people in target accounts, becoming more effective at doing so will improve your chances of reaching an appropriate decision maker and obtaining a good outcome in the form of a job or referral.

The Internet has fueled the growth of these tools, leveling the playing field for all who are willing to put in the effort. Like anything online, there are other sources we've not yet uncovered or used. But these tools can be a big help to finding new potential contacts, influencers, and even hiring authorities to add to your growing personal social network.

Two such tools are www.Jigsaw.com and www.NetProspex.com.

Unlike the general-purpose LinkedIn, there is a small cost to access the above databases—$25 per month at last look. But you can sign up for a month, do your research on any number of companies, and then end your subscription. You can always jump back in later in three months if you need this service again.

The beauty of these tools is their simplicity. For example, if you want to find out if there is a VP of Sales in Company X, simply type in the company name and the appropriate job title, and see what comes up.

The results might be one or several individuals or none at all. And they may or may not be whom you are looking for. This functions just like a Google search, only with far greater precision.

You also could expand your search to all potential hiring "managers" by typing in that term. You may find HR managers, staffing managers, or sales managers. It's a broader group, but you may discover related hiring authorities or influencers in other parts of the company by doing that sort of search.

Lead Generation Tools Are Fluid

These three resources are highly fluid and changing. As with LinkedIn and other social networks, new members join everyday.

Jigsaw and NetProspex contacts are "user generated." This means that people who use these tools to find leads are able to add, to change, and to update the information, including adding new contacts they have as well as changing the status, titles, phone, and e-mail contact information as they come across it. As a result, the information you can find here is changing and growing all the time. You may not find a contact you need today, but next week or month, there may be five you will find there.

Being user generated, not all the information is up to date. Just like you, people leave companies, change jobs, or get promotions.

So, yes, although you pay for each name you download—Jigsaw charges $1 per name—and get access to their contact information (phone number and e-mail address), the information you seek does not always pan out.

Be advised that the contact information may not always be accurate. The phone number may be the main company number. The e-mail address may no longer work or be valid. The contact may have left the company altogether. But in those cases in which you get a dud, just update the Jigsaw database, and you'll get a credit. Simple enough.

When starting from ground zero with few to no contacts in a company, having the ability to find people at your target companies who might be of help to you in your search is huge. That's the value of lead generation tools, such as Jigsaw and NetProspex.

Jigsaw versus NetProspex

Jigsaw has been around longer, while NetProspex is more of a newcomer but growing fast. One of the best elements of NetProspex is that its data is kept current. Its approach is to do as much work as possible to verify the accuracy of the contacts in its database. It also focuses on not having any lead older than two years back.

Unlike Jigsaw, where you will find contacts that were created and inputted by someone anywhere from today to several years ago, NetProspex leads are more current. Therefore, this site can be a more accurate source of lead contact information. However, it's a newer site, so it does not have the several million contacts you can access on the Jigsaw database. NetProspex will catch up, though.

Remember that like any database, the information is never 100 percent identical. Sure, there will be overlap. More current information overlap is a good thing. And finding new folks in one database who were not in another is even better.

Other Research Tools

Our objective here is to give you a few good resources that can help you start building your personal social network.

There are many other places to look, too. Some of these other resources include the obvious, such as search engines.

1. Corporate Web sites, Press Releases, News Archives
Don't discount visiting corporate Web sites. See if they have "Press Releases/News Archives" sections. This can be a useful source of information to mine and can turn up influencers or people in decision-making roles, simply because those are the types of people usually quoted in articles/press releases.

It takes time to read or to scan through this sort of stuff, but, again, this is part of your research. There is no easy way around research. Once you've done a bit of experimenting with it, you will come to appreciate its value.

2. Trade Publications

Every industry or market has one or sometimes several key trade/ magazine publications. If you're in the industry, you can often get what's called a "controlled circulation" subscription for free. Simply fill out the "bingo card" and mail it in or fill it in online.

Better yet, check with your local main public library or university, and see which ones they may subscribe to. It's often just the "main" ones in larger markets, but you never know. And it doesn't cost you a dime. Ask for the business librarian if the library has one, as he or she will be more in tune with that aspect of his or her periodicals…which is what these publications are called.

In addition to being a solid source of information on a specific market, many times these periodicals have "People in the News" sections about recent promotions and job changes. Look there, and read through these articles as a potential source for finding possible influencers and hiring authorities to add your personal social network.

And with many publications now putting their content online, do some research to see which ones may offer you free online access.

8

Social Media Channels: The Online Happy Hour

S OCIAL MEDIA HAS BECOME THE NEW WAY to rapidly increase your professional and personal networks via user-generated content through such channels as podcasting, commenting and posting in forums geared to your area(s) of expertise, and writing and submitting articles (e.g., short pieces and longer, more in-depth articles, or even white papers if you're so inclined). The content that you generate should be centered on your professional interests, experience, and industry. It's tweeting, YouTubing, and vertical social networking. And each of these opportunities is available to you for your job search.

Social media represents the myriad of vehicles that allow you to virtually connect to, to communicate with, and to build/nurture your social network and to successfully conduct a social networking campaign.

To sum up the essence:

- Social networks are massive groups of potential network contacts.
- Social networking is the "reaching out."
- Social media channels are how you do it.

You can opt for using only one or two social media channels to stay connected, or you may get hooked, like many have, and become a social networking and media junkie, blogging several times a day and wanting to use as many ways as possible to stay in touch with your growing social network of professional contacts.

That's the beauty behind social media. It's completely creative; it's totally up to you. It's totally individual, totally tailored by you and for you based on your interests and the time you choose to put into staying in touch and building as well as nurturing your network.

Social media is the glue that binds together your commitment to maintain your social networking. It's how to stay in touch, however you choose to do so.

> JOB SEEKER SUCCESS STORY:
> New to Facebook? No Worries!
>
> Brent Vaughn, 40, was going through some very tough times in 2009. A resident of the Nashville, Tennessee, suburbs, Vaughn not only lost his job as a supervisor but was going through a divorce that forced him to move back in with his parents. He needed to find work quickly.
>
> Vaughn's sister suggested he set up a profile on Facebook to make some contacts although he knew very little about using the social network. Within a few days of setting up the account and profile, a friend referred him to a company that was seeking a manager. In a

matter of a couple weeks, Vaughn had an interview and was hired for the position.

"Every time I tell someone I found a job through Facebook, they are amazed," Vaughn says. "I was basically a rookie at it."

With millions of users, sites like the popular Facebook can be crucial in slimming down the time it takes between losing a job and finding a new position. If there is not a direct connection, these sites can serve to point job seekers in the right direction.

Vaughn, luckily, had a sister experienced with online networking sites and was able to take advantage of the resource in his quest for work. By using the site, Vaughn had the help of his friends keeping a lookout for a position he might be able to fill.

These networks are becoming increasingly effective in job searches throughout the country and are another tool in the box to conduct a comprehensive search.

SOURCE: Lindberg, Joseph, and Ojeda-Zapata, Julio. "Facebook, Twitter, LinkedIn Can Lead to Jobs for Unemployed." *St. Paul Pioneer Press,* 18 October 2009.

Regardless of your present employment situation, people searching via social networks and social media channels will be key. Remember, the old way of going about getting a job via the traditional job search may not be dead, but it certainly is being usurped by people searching or the use of social networks.

This may not seem like such a big deal, but it is, in fact, a dramatic shift. With this approach, the focus shifts from being about the job to focusing on building and developing relationships with an ever-widening "personal power social network." This is why you need to think not of a "job search" but of a "people search" as the mentality that will land you a job faster.

The phenomenon of social networks has become more mainstream over the past several years. Such retail giants as Target, Dell, and many other large corporate firms are jumping into the space at an ever increasing pace. Yet we believe social networking is still in its infancy when it comes to the importance and value of people searching for career needs and interests.

Certainly, members of generations X and Y (individuals ranging in age from 18 to 45) have been the early adopters of these networks. As a result, these demographic groups have reaped the benefit of career enhancement and mobility more quickly than other parts of the population.

By jumping on the social networks/social media bandwagon sooner rather than later and immersing yourself in this incredibly exciting world, you'll gain a huge edge on your competition for career opportunities in the marketplace.

We can't emphasize it enough: It doesn't matter if your need for a career change is immediate or far in the future. Whether your mentality is "I've got to get a paycheck right away" or a more casual "I just want to know what interesting challenges might come up," you *always* need to be positioning yourself for the next job.

Learning to use and to incorporate all the tools of social networking into your people search and, even more importantly, continuing to develop it *after* you're happily and newly settled is something you can't afford *not* to take advantage of.

9

Interviewing Considerations

SOCIAL MEDIA IS FAST BECOMING the most popular forum for employers and job seekers to meet. In a recent study conducted by CareerBuilder.com, it was found that nearly 22 percent of employers regularly review profiles on the social networking sites when in search of candidates for available openings. It was also found that an additional 9 percent of employers plan to add this method to their current recruitment efforts.

Many of the employers in the CareerBuilder.com survey said they review networking sites in order to gain a sense of the person behind the profile or resume. Employers want to identify possible matches not solely in terms of skill set and experience but to gauge if there might be a cultural fit as well.

On the candidate side, social media sites permit users to create profiles that can also serve as an online resume. Knowing what employers are looking for when perusing the sites will help candidates understand that creating a professional and unique image will enhance their candidacy. As described in Chapter 2, it is through personal branding that you can differentiate your candidacy from others in the job market. Because the goal of job search is to garner an interview, any method that allows you to stand apart from the crowd is well worth the time and effort.

Your personal brand is built upon your core strengths and competencies. Many of us may be good communicators or have strong sales ability, but it is in how you package these skills to reflect your unique style that reflects your brand. So let's apply what we learned earlier about branding into how you will strategize for a job interview.

Profile Branding and Interview Strategy

Just as a resume and cover letter have been your first introduction to potential employers in a traditional job search, your profile serves as the first introduction in a social media search.

As with corporate branding, the goal of personal branding is to foster an impression of consistency and reliability. In light of this, be sure that the image you convey in your profile follows through to the image you present in any interview, whether on the phone or face to face.

Visual branding refers to how you dress, walk, gesture, or approach someone to shake his or her hand. In essence, your visual brand is your overall style and how you create a unique look. This also refers to the colors you choose for your job search marketing material (e.g., resume, cover letter, thank-you letter). Each element should match in terms of color, texture, and overall style.

Visual branding should also be reflected in your social media content with regard to the picture you post to your profile, your posture, and facial expression along with the colors you choose for your clothing. If you can include a background color in your profile, it should match the color of your resume, cover letter, and any other materials.

During any face-to-face job interview, ensure that your clothing matches in the style and, ideally, color that you wore for your profile shot. If your body posture in the picture gave off an approachable style with a warm smile, be sure to replicate this attitude during any interviews. Smile as you are introduced to the interviewer; lean forward slightly as you shake hands.

If the first interview will be a phone screen, you can still convey a warm attitude by smiling as you talk and speaking in a low volume with a slow and measured cadence. Don't rush; give the interviewer a chance to digest what you are saying.

JOB SEEKER SUCCESS STORY:
Know Your Way Around Social Media? Your Interview Has Begun.

Ryan May, a 33-year-old vice president at Risdall McKinney Public Relations in New Brighton, Minnesota, had been involved with social networking sites for six years before landing his job with LinkedIn.

"Social media allow you to promote yourself as a good employee and a possible asset to a company," May says. "Whatever tools you have at your disposal, you should use to the best of your ability."

Besides using the professional networking LinkedIn site and contacts there to snag his job, May also operated an account on Twitter, the brief status update site. Users can post brief 140-character updates in real time that are broadcast to all the users' followers. He also operates the Minnesota Public Relations blog, which posts job openings in the state each week.

May attributes his success in getting his job to keeping connected on LinkedIn, the company that was in a position to eventually hire him.

Due to his several years of experience with these social networking sites, May also cautions job candidates regarding what potential employers may find on their profiles. "Facebook and MySpace are easy to botch up," May says, "because you can get caught on (those) doing something you shouldn't be doing."

Many employers are growing aware of these types of sites and will check on job candidates' profiles before hiring them. A majority said they found photos, comments, and other issues on these sites that caused them not to pursue candidates.

May says users should think carefully about what they post on the sites due to the potential consequences, especially when looking for employment.

SOURCE: Lindberg, Joseph, and Ojeda-Zapata, Julio. "Facebook, Twitter, LinkedIn Can Lead to Jobs for Unemployed." *St. Paul Pioneer Press,* 18 October 2009.

Written Communication

Written communication refers to the marketing message you create to convey your unique skills and abilities. This description will play a key part of your profile description. If you incorporate a resume-like profile, your brand will be evident in the way you compose your career summary, as well as in the way you order and word your past accomplishments.

Although a resume is somewhat technical in nature, all other job-search correspondence, such as profile descriptions, cover letters, and follow-up letters, should convey the same tone. If your brand is "approachable and warm," then your writing should reflect this mood but not be overly familiar or incorporate slang language.

As potential employers peruse your resume or profile, they will be looking to see if the wording and phrasing matches the visual impression they have obtained from your photo and other images. Any dissonance may give them pause in pursuing things further.

For example, dressing conservatively in your photo but using slang terminology in your profile might raise a red flag for a recruiter.

It is often the case that the interview process involves the completion of an application. Use the same wording and terminology on the application that you used on your resume. Be sure the dates of employment and school attendance match, as the interviewer may well take some time to review each in a side-by-side manner.

Do not place the words "See Resume" under the "Job Responsibilities" section. Take the time to complete the application in full. Go slowly to avoid mistakes. If you do make one, place one line through the text, and make the correction above.

If the interview process includes the submission of a writing sample, be sure to write in the same tone in which you composed all your other job search material.

Add Professional Groups and Fan Pages

It will benefit your job search if you join groups or add pages that show evidence of civic or professional engagement. These groups also can reflect your well-rounded interests. These may be industry associations, trade groups, hobby and sports clubs, or volunteer activities. Join only those groups or pages in which you have an authentic interest and genuinely reflect the brand you wish to develop. Employers like to hire staff who participate in diverse activities and have active social lives. As a result, this may well be a subject that comes up at some point during the interview, so be prepared to talk in some detail about the groups and/or pages you have joined.

Preparing for the Face-to-Face Interview

Throughout this book, we've devoted a great deal of attention to how social media is an indispensable means for job seekers when it comes to making connections and creating interview opportunities. Earlier in this chapter, we emphasize the need for consistency between your social profile and how you present yourself in person.

All that said, it would be a terrible shame to invest weeks, months, and years of making connections by not being able to capitalize on them with a fantastic face-to-face interview. Unfortunately, this is all too common. When we speak to recruiters, we are told that an amazingly high number of candidates interview poorly. This is even true of highly educated and experienced individuals. Recruiters report that many candidates simply don't know how to prepare for an interview. They expect the recruiter to do the heavy lifting of making connections between the candidates' qualifications and the job at hand.

It often seems as if many folks have the notion that all you need to do for an interview is to show up on time, to dress and to behave nicely, and to answer questions off the top of your head as best you can. In a tough job market, that doesn't cut it. So here are some helpful tips when it comes to preparing for a face-to-face interview:

1. *Use your contacts to help you prepare for the interview.*
   Too many times, candidates prepare by doing no more than checking out the company's Web site. Think about it: If the contacts that you've made through social media and in person have such an impact in ensuring that you get an interview, just imagine how helpful they can be in preparing for your interview!

If you have a good contact with a company, you may very well be able to obtain some invaluable inside info on the job. Here are some questions you can ask in advance:

1. "I'm interviewing with Mr. X in Department Y. Do you know anyone I could talk to who knows Mr. X or what it's like to work in Department Y?"
2. "What kind of person tends to be a good fit for this organization?"
3. "What do employees like most and least about working in this group?"
4. "Do you know anything about how the interview process usually works with this manager or with this company in general?"

At worst, showing that you did some homework prior to the interview will reflect positively on you as a proactive individual who really wants the job. At best, you may obtain some information that leads you to change your strategic focus dramatically or perhaps even to know what you'll be asked in advance!

2. *Spend more time on researching the job description than you do on researching the company.*
You may or may not get asked a question to see how well you really understand what the company does and what the job entails. Obviously, you need to have a fundamental idea of the organization's mission. Asking such a question as, "So what is it that you actually *do* here?" can be the death knell for the unprepared candidate.

However, job seekers who spend hours poring over a company's facts and figures and managing to memorize them are investing a ton of energy in doing the wrong thing the right way. Unless you're applying to be a chief financial officer of a company, you probably don't really need to know the exact amount of revenues or profits that company reaped last year. If you're going after an accounting position, memorizing the whole product line won't really help.

It's far better to invest your precious time in researching the job description itself. Do you *really* understand every term and each software application mentioned on it? If not, you'd better do some work. Let's say that an information technology job description says that "Knowledge of Symantec Ghost is preferred."

Who would you rather hire: the candidate who says "I know nothing about Symantec Ghost, but I'm willing to learn," or the job seeker who says, "I haven't had the opportunity to work with Ghost, but from my research I know that it's an application that is useful when you're attempting to migrate an end user from an old machine to a new one without making him or her redo his or her desktop configuration from scratch."

3. *Prepare a notes page if you fear blanking out.*
   Some candidates worry that they will suddenly go blank in the middle of an interview due to nerves. Even if that's not the case, it's not a bad idea to have one page of notes in front of you during the interview. Here are some pointers:

- Make the font quite large, so you can glance at them without minimizing eye contact.
- Having notes makes you seem more prepared… unless you read them, which has the opposite effect. Keep them simple.
- Your notes should include three or four strategic selling points, supporting stories for those points, key research that you want to incorporate, and great questions you want to ask at the end.
- Limit your notes to one side of one page to avoid distracting the interviewer by flipping pages.

4. *Develop a preinterview routine that gets you into the right mindset.*

This can vary dramatically from one individual to the next. If you're the kind of person who gets nervous, the best idea is to embrace and to welcome that nervous energy rather than fighting to stay calm. Nervousness is just energy, so *use it* to project enthusiasm and to focus closely on what the interviewer is saying.

Another idea would be to exercise vigorously a few hours before the interview if possible. Others may prefer calming meditation. Either way, you can simultaneously visualize the interview, focusing on how you well address various questions that are likely to arise. If you envision yourself feeling confident and doing well, you are more likely to make that a reality when the moment comes.

5. *Spend time in advance planning how to answer questions that are likely to arise.*

   You should never be surprised to hear any of these questions:

   - Tell me about yourself.
   - Why should we hire you for this job?
   - What are your strengths?
   - What are your weaknesses?
   - Where do you see yourself in five years?
   - Tell me about some of your top accomplishments in your last job.

You should have answers ready to go for any of these straightforward questions. Bear in mind, though, that HOW you answer each question may vary dramatically from one interview to the next. Whether it's an open-ended question or a specific one, the REAL question is ALWAYS, "Why are YOU a good match for THIS job?"

Many candidates just don't get this. If you're applying for a job in which you'll be sitting by yourself in a cubicle all day—or out on the road as a sales rep working a territory—then why say that "being a team player" is one of your strengths? If you're applying for a job with a Fortune 100 company, it's not going to do you any good to announce that you see yourself working as a consultant in five years. Although you always need to be honest, you always want to provide answers that show that you are a fit for the job at hand.

Many candidates fear the weaknesses question. The main idea is to offer an honest but nonfatal weakness. For example, a software developer could admit to a lack of confidence when it comes to public-speaking skills. A marketing professional could acknowledge that her computer skills are solid but that she lacks advanced knowledge of sophisticated databases, such as SAP or Oracle.

The Interview Itself

Once you have done a great job with your research and preparation, the next goal is to execute your strategy as well as possible when you interview. So let's consider the variables that will be important to master here.

The most important parts of the interview are the beginning and the ending, as those are the segments that the employer will remember best. This is bad news for many candidates. Ironically, most candidates are at their worst at the beginning and end of the interview!

What are the reasons for this unfortunate phenomenon? Certainly nervousness is high at the beginning of an interview, and a nervous candidate is also eager to rush through the ending of the interview instead of using it as an opportunity to take control of the conversation.

That said, a bigger factor is inadequate preparation. At the beginning of an interview, candidates are usually asked open-ended questions about themselves or their strengths. If the candidate hasn't prepared a strategy—and doesn't know to look for an oppor-tunity to deliver it as early as possible—then a simple question, such as, "Tell me about yourself," becomes an impossibly broad question to answer.

If, on the other hand, you have a keen awareness of your personal brand and how it fits into the requirements of the job at hand, then you will start to *hope* for these open-ended questions, as they will give you an early opportunity to provide a handful of reasons why you're a good match for the job.

Verbal Branding

Verbal branding refers to how you communicate orally in terms of both content and style: the words you choose to use and your manner of speaking, including your pitch, tone, and cadence.

Any consideration of content ties back to the creation of an "elevator pitch," which we mention earlier as well as the strategy formulation that we just described. As a reminder, this is your 30-second introduction of "brand you." It would include what job you currently hold (or last held), what type of job you are seeking, and your three greatest strengths in the context of the job that you want. The message should be no longer than three lines and needs to capture your skills and abilities along with the value you bring to a new employer. Have it handy for any telephone interviews. It will be best to highlight keywords that will trigger your memory so that you may speak naturally rather than sound as if you are reading off a card.

If you did not have a prescreening interview, or if you are connecting with someone at a job fair or networking event, you can use this pitch to answer the all-but-inevitable question, "Tell me something about yourself" when in a face-to-face meeting.

During either a telephone or face-to-face interview, the potential employer will be paying close attention to ensure that there is a match between what you stated in your resume or profile and what you are saying during the discussion. Perhaps there is no other area where branding is as important as with the creation of a unified message. There definitely needs to be consistency between the words you use in speech and those you incorporate into any written correspondence.

Although articulating strong content is obviously vital, don't underestimate the importance of style when it comes to delivering your message. The biggest problem that recruiters usually see is with *pace*. Many interviewees simply talk too fast. Sometimes this is due to nerves, but it also can be a case of the interviewee speaking at the same pace he or she would use in a freewheeling conversation with a friend. Remember that it's hard to be an INTERVIEWER! All at once, the interviewer needs to listen, to assess your answer, to decide whether to ask a follow-up question, to take notes, and to act in an engaging manner.

With all that going on, you are doing the interviewer—and yourself—a favor by slowing down and even pausing, especially after making a powerful point. Give the interviewer the chance to digest and to reflect, and don't fret if there are periods of silence.

Beyond pace, the other key with verbal style is to avoid monotony. Show your enthusiasm for the job by making sure that your voice conveys excitement. Vary your pace—speeding up slightly when giving background information but slowing down when describing an accomplishment or some other "moment of truth."

Creating Rapport

It's very easy for a candidate to maintain an internal focus throughout an interview. The interviewee can become quite self-absorbed as he or she thinks about what he or she wants to say next. Although this is natural, the risk is that the candidate sometimes fails to really pay attention to the interviewer and to build rapport.

There are many ways to build rapport during an interview. If you are escorted into an office and see a diploma, a plaque, a book, or a momento from a favorite sports team, it may give you a nice conversational opening. This is especially true if you have an alma mater, professional association, or hobby in common. Of course, advance study of a LinkedIn site might give you insight into these areas, too. Either way, find a way to connect with the interviewer.

During the interview, you can build rapport by actively listening to questions. Sometimes asking a clarifying question can buy time while showing you are really engaged in the conversation. If the interviewer goes on a tangent, you sometimes have to be prepared to roll with that and to show that your focus is sharp. Keep an eye out for nonverbal reactions as you speak: You may be able to tell when your points are hitting the mark and when they are met with indifference.

Earning Credibility

There is a fine line in an interview between selling yourself as strongly as you can versus overselling yourself. Don't make any claim that you can't back up, as doing so will raise questions about how valid ANY of your alleged strengths are. On the other hand, don't sell yourself short. Some candidates go out of their way to minimize their accomplishments. Be honest about what you can and cannot do.

This is especially true with computer skills. If you are claiming to be proficient in Excel on your resume or in your interview, then you certainly better know at least SOME advanced functions, such as vlookup, macros, and pivots as well as formulas, charts, and graphs. If you only know the latter, maybe you'd better describe yourself as "familiar with" Excel.

Opportunities to Inject PAR Formulas

Remember those PAR formulas that you worked on developing a few chapters ago? A great piece of advice is to seek opportunities to inject your best PAR formulas into any interview.

If you've done your homework in creating succinct and powerful formulas, this may be relatively easy or somewhat difficult, depending on the interviewer's style. In the best-case scenario, you may be asked some *behavioral-based interviewing* questions. Here are some examples:

- Tell me specifically what your greatest accomplishment was in your last job.
- Tell me about a specific time when you had to overcome a challenge while working in a group.
- Describe a situation in which you had to take an unpopular stand.

These questions are asking you to give a step-by-step description of specific behaviors that you demonstrated in past circumstances. Why do employers ask such questions? Because they want you to PROVE that you really have a specific skill or trait rather than just CLAIMING you do.

This format is good news for candidates who have developed several good PAR formulas. A good behavioral-based interviewing story generally starts with a problem and shows the actions that you took to reach a specific result. If you have four or five PAR formulas ready to use, a behavioral interview will be much easier.

Even in a conventional interview, look for opportunities to inject your PAR formulas into your answers. If you're asked about your strengths or about a past job, it will be to your advantage to take those open-ended questions and to answer them with the nitty-gritty specifics of a PAR formula. With those details, the interviewer will see that you're not just conveniently claiming that your greatest strengths just happen to be the qualifications that the company lists on the job description.

Do Not Disparage Current Employers

A common interview question is in regard to what you think of your current employer, supervisor, or co-workers. This is not the time to complain that you were given an unfair performance evaluation during your last review or to indicate any form of disgruntlement. To answer a question of this nature, speak in neutral terms with something along the lines of, "I admire and get along well with everyone in my current firm and know I will miss them when I leave."

It will do your brand (and job search) no good to speak negatively about current or past employers. Making disparaging remarks may only serve to instill the impression that you are a whiner or malcontent who will one day talk negatively about whoever hires you. That can end your candidacy right there.

Managing the Q&A Section

For the better part of the interview, the interviewer determines what happens. Eventually, though, the interviewer will give you the opportunity to take command of the interview. This usually happens at the end, when you will be asked if you have any questions.

The worst thing you can do is to say, "No, thanks; I'm all set." This actually happens pretty often, as some candidates are just eager to have the interview over. Yet this is a major mistake, as foregoing questions is basically akin to saying that you really aren't that interested in the job.

You always want to ask at least two or three questions at the end of the interview and perhaps as many as five or six depending on how much information the interviewer disclosed during the interview.

Here are some useful tips to keep in mind when it comes to questions and answers:

1. *Ask questions that show off your research.*

   If you didn't have an opportunity to showcase the sweat equity that you put into preparation, now is the time to make that happen. You might ask a question that shows you are aware of a product in the pipeline or that reveals that you went out of your way to talk to other employees at the organization. Just don't throw them under the bus if they revealed anything negative to you!

2. *Ask questions that show positive values.*

   Now is not the time to ask about vacation time, benefits, and how late you can arrive at work each day. Instead, ask about what you could do to be considered a top performer in the role. Ask questions that show intellectual curiosity about the organization's products or services. Ask what other work you would be able to take on if you prove you are efficient and effective in getting your primary tasks done.

3. *Listen to how your question is answered, and REACT to it.* Typically, candidates treat the Q&A section as a mandatory exercise that is not particularly interesting to them. They ask a question, get an answer, and say, "Oh, okay. Another question I have is." Instead, show that you were listening and react to the answer, seizing an opportunity to show why you're a good fit. Here's an example:

Candidate: "What could I do to be considered a top performer in this role?"

Interviewer: "Well, obviously we need someone who has great attention to detail, given that this is a bookkeeping role. However, I would say that the *best* performers here are also those who are low-maintenance employees. Our attitude is that there is plenty of 'task stress' here; we don't want a lot of 'people stress' too."

Candidate: "That's great to hear. Attention to detail is a real strength, and I definitely pride myself on being an employee who makes life easier for my manager and co-workers by having a positive attitude and being willing to chip in when things are busy. If you want to call my last manager, I'm sure she'll tell you that I was always calm under pressure."

The goal is to transform the Q&A section from a perfunctory exercise into a purpose-driven dialogue. This will help you end your interview on a high note.

4. *Always move to the conclusion by asking about next steps.*
   When you are done asking questions about the job itself, you'll want to ask about next steps: "My only other question would be this: When do you plan to make a hiring decision?" Whatever the interviewer says, you can say, "Great. Shall I await word from you, or should I touch base with a call or an e-mail?" Ask for a business card so you'll be prepared to send a thank-you note.

5. *Finish up by summarizing why you're a good fit for the job.*
   After you're clear on what will happen next, you'll want to express your appreciation for the opportunity to interview and to summarize your strategic position as to why you're a good fit for the job. You also may incorporate things you learned during the interview: "I just want to say thanks for having me in today to learn more about this opportunity. I think that if you're looking for someone who has great attention to detail, good bookkeeping experience, and who is definitely a low-maintenance employee, then I'm sure I'd be a great fit for your position."

After the Interview

Even after the interview is over, there is still another opportunity for you to help or to harm your chances of obtaining the job. In a great economy for job seekers, a thank-you note is still a good idea. Believe it or not, though, a thank-you note can make the difference between getting an offer and not getting one—particularly in a tight economy.

These days, it's not unusual for managers to receive dozens of resumes in response to a job listing. If you were one of the few who used social media and other networking skills to get your foot in the door, good for you. Regardless, though, we hear of managers these days who report that they narrowed a field of 100+ candidates down to four or five finalists—all of whom were great people who could do the job. So how do they pick just one?

These days, it often comes down to little things. If everyone is obviously qualified to do the job, it might be a matter of who is most likely to stay in the position the longest. It could be a case of whoever did the best job of creating a personal connection with the manager. And it might even be the case of who wrote the most personal, timely, and error-free thank-you note after the interview.

A handwritten thank-you note is more personal, but a typed thank-you e-mail is timelier. Do either, but get that message out right away, and make sure that it's perfectly worded. Sending a message fraught with awkward phraseology or typos is worse than not sending one at all.

In Sum: Be Prepared

The best time to review your profile is *before* you launch a job-search campaign. In this way, you will be able to remove any questionable content before a potential employer has the opportunity to see it. As a litmus test when editing your profile, ask yourself whether the content you wish to post is something you would be comfortable having a potential employer read. If not, remove it. As they say, you only get one chance to make a great first impression!

Likewise, the best time to show how qualified you are for a job is *before* the interview. You usually will not know how tough the interviewer will be, and you almost never know how much competition you'll be facing. You always have to assume that you're going up against strong candidates and that you will need to outwork them when it comes to research and preparation, particularly strategizing. It's a bad feeling to come out of an interview knowing in your heart that you weren't as prepared as you might've been.

Conversely, it's a great feeling to know that you did your very best. If you did your best but don't get the job, then you have to accept what is beyond your control. You may do everything right but come up against a candidate who has better experience or a stronger personal connection to the decision maker. But if you keep going the extra mile with research and preparation, eventually you'll get a good offer—maybe even beating out someone who is much stronger on paper!

PART III

Landing

10

Negotiation 2.0

THE PRIMARY MESSAGE you tried to instill in the minds of employers throughout your job search was your value to the company. To be successful with the offer negotiation process, you must first understand how that value translates into a monetary figure.

Research Comparable Salaries

The first step is to obtain some reliable salary figures for someone with your skill set, experience, industry, and geographic region. There are many resources available on the Web (such as Salary. com), in business libraries, and through your business network that can provide you with comparable salary information. Although it is unlikely that you will find an exact salary for your particular situation, the more research you conduct, the more confident you will become that the salary you quote will be realistic and present a "fair-market value" for your skills and accomplishments.

Relying on multiple sources for salary information means that you will obtain a fairly accurate picture of the range for your profession, years of experience, and current job-market trends with regard to your industry.

In deciding on an appropriate salary range, don't forget to factor in the "opportunity cost" of leaving your current position in terms of any commissions due, year-end bonuses, annual review, pay raises, or stock options not yet vested.

After you analyze your findings, you will create three levels of salary:

- **Your "Bottom Line" Number**: This is the lowest salary you will accept in order to meet your financial responsibilities while allowing you to work toward your longer range career and lifestyle goals.
- **Your "Comfort Zone" Number**: This is the salary at which you believe you will be adequately compensated in terms of the title and responsibilities of the position. This figure will also permit you to live comfortably in a manner to which you are accustomed.
- **Your "Ideal" Number**: This is the level of salary earned by top performers in your field.

Negotiating an Offer

Now that you have the three sets of numbers laid out, it's time to lay out a strategy for when an employment offer is actually made. When an employer offers you a given salary or quotes a salary range, your initial research will tell you if the number is too low, too high, or on target.

Many companies that offer impressive benefits packages may attempt to persuade you accept a lower salary. Only you can decide what will be best for yourself, your family, your career, and current situation. Keep in mind that if you accept a lower salary now, it will affect the amount of increases you obtain as you move forward with the company, because pay raises are based on a percentage of current salary.

Negotiating When the Offer Is Too Low

When an offer is too low, your initial response might be to repeat the number in a nonjudgmental tone and then stop talking. During this interval, you will be comparing this number to your "Bottom Line" figure. If the salary offered does not fall within even this bottom level, a possible response might be:

"Ms. Smith, thank you for the offer. I am truly appreciative that you believe I am the right person for this job and excited about getting started in meeting the challenges we discussed."

Then clarify:

"Please allow me to clarify my understanding of the position. This is a full-time, exempt position as IT division manager for your Cincinnati office. I would be reporting to the vice president of Technology and be responsible for the supervision of seven staff. I would be required to manage the implementations of new technological initiatives within the branch office during the first six months of employment and spearhead some cost-cutting measures to trim at least 15 percent off the department budget.

"Do I have this correct?"

Make a strong case for a higher salary based on the value you will bring to the role. Be sure to mention any critical needs discussed during the interview and your ability to solve those issue:

"As we discussed, I have the requisite skill set to make an immediate contribution. As you know, I have led the successful implementation of new equipment in my current role and feel confident of my ability to reproduce that success with this company. Based on my expected contributions and what I have come to understand to be fair-market value from some industry-based research for this level of position, a salary range of X to Y would be more appropriate. Can you work with me in this range?"

Three Possible Responses from the Employer

1. Employer doesn't budge.
   Suggested response:
   Remain enthusiastic and display an attitude of cooperation: You want to give the impression that you are trying to work out a win-win situation:

   "Okay, I do understand your position. I remain confident in my ability to excel in this role, so perhaps we can build in some performance-based bonuses? I would certainly also factor in the scope of the benefits package offered."

2. Employer raises the offer a bit but still below your expectations.
   Remain positive, and reiterate key challenges of the position. Once again, express your confidence that you can meet and exceed performance expectations:

   "I remember our discussion about the difficulty the department is having with team morale and how it is

adversely affecting productivity. I have a consistent history of building strong teams in very similar situations, and I have full confidence in my ability to drive consensus and to enhance overall productivity. I have calculated that even a 5 percent boost in productivity would increase your bottom line by $50,000 in the first year alone. Based on this assessment, could you agree that a salary range of X and Y would be fair?"

Continue on in this vein as long as the employer is receptive and you are able to continue documenting relevant past experience. As in the above example, it is always helpful to translate your value in terms of hard numbers.

3. Employer counters with an offer that is aligned with your needs and expectations.

The negotiation process is now over, and you can move forward to discussing benefits, bonuses, and special perks.

Negotiating Additional Elements of Compensation Package

Although base salary is usually the most significant aspect of offer negotiation, there are other considerations that should play a role in whether you accept the offer. For example, if the proffered salary is within your "ideal" range, but the company does not contribute substantially to health insurance coverage, you will need to factor in your out-of-pocket expenses for adequate coverage for yourself or you and your family.

If the salary is below your expectations, but you remain interested in the position, you may be able to negotiate health and other benefits. Keep in mind that the hiring manager may not have the authority to make decisions in this regard but should be able to speak on your behalf with the appropriate department manager(s).

Additional Compensation/Performance Evaluations/Bonuses/Commissions

- You may be able to negotiate a lesser period of time for initial evaluation, thereby obtaining a salary increase in less time than is normal policy.
- Ask whether there is an option to add performance-based bonuses and, if so, how often they might be granted.
- If your position is sales based, ask about the commission structure and whether there is a cap. Can you receive residual commission income from past sales?
- Inquire whether the company has a profit-sharing plan and how much the company matches? Can you negotiate the amount you and/or the company contribute?
- Will you be provided with a company BlackBerry and/or laptop, and, if so, what are the restrictions on its use? Will you need to be on call 24/7?

Benefits

- What is the vacation policy? Can you negotiate for more paid time off?
- What is the cost of health insurance, and how much does the company contribute? Can you negotiate a higher contribution from the company in lieu of a lower starting salary?

- Are dental and vision coverage provided? If the cost is extra, is there an option to obtain this coverage at no or reduced cost in exchange for accepting a lower salary?
- Does the company have a tuition assistance program? Can the amount of assistance be increased if you accept the lower salary?

Social Media and Job Offers

Social media has come to be an important component of company policy in recent years. It is important to keep in mind that employers have the right to monitor your business and personal profiles on social media sites to discover if you have violated security or confidentiality. Writing disparaging comments about your company on any personal Web page, blog, or social media profile can result in serious consequences, including possible loss of employment. Some candidates have even had offers rescinded for writing negative blogs about an employer before the first day of work!

During the negotiation process, you may be curious as to the company's policy with regard to any number of issues, including the use of the Internet and social media in the workplace. However, it's important to differentiate between "nice-to-know" information versus "need-to-know" issues. The aforementioned questions on benefits are certainly "need-to-know" elements of any job offer. Additionally, seeking clarity on whether the company requires a signed noncompete agreement might be advisable.

As for social media and the use of the Internet in general, there are plenty of great questions about social media that are bound to arise eventually. However, unless your position is specifically related to social media, we recommend that you hold off on asking such questions until *after* you are hired. Even then, proceed with caution. As you are building good relationships with your new colleagues, you'll want to focus on being a top performer. Asking many questions about the use of social media may raise some questions about your priorities as a new employee.

That said, here are some questions that you should explore at your workplace, even if only through informal dialogue:

- How does the company define social media?
- How does the company use social media for marketing and networking?
- If I create a personal Web site or blog or answer personal e-mail on any company-owned equipment (e.g. office computer, laptop, or BlackBerry), will I retain copyright to the content if I leave the company?
- Are there limitations regarding the content of what I write on my personal page or blog with regard to the company?
- Do I need to sign a confidentiality agreement regarding any aspect of the company's products, services, or proprietary information?
- Are employees encouraged to create social media accounts (e.g., Twitter) to interact with current and potential customers? To network with colleagues?
- Does the company offer training with regard to the proper use of social media?
- Is a manual provided that covers social media policy?
- Is it okay to use the Internet occasionally for personal use? If so, what is really acceptable in terms of Internet use?
- Are there any restrictions with regard to access to certain social media sites (e.g., YouTube)?
- How is the use of social media regulated by the company?

- What actions does the company take against an employee who violates the company's social media policy?

JOB SEEKER SUCCESS STORY:
Finding Work on LinkedIn Alone

Cate Phillips, 30, of Milwaukee, Wisconsin, put all her job-search eggs in one basket and only used the social networking site LinkedIn to find a job.

"The only reason I have my current job is because of LinkedIn," Phillips says. "I used no other tool, and I did not reach out in any other way."

Phillips did nothing other than change her employment status on the professional networking site. She said she asked contacts she previously had on the site for recommendations.

Friends and other contacts from the site, including former co-workers, started helping her in her job search. She said she even received help from someone on the site she did not know. Phillips began attending several immediate interviews and was hired as a vice president of sales and marketing within two months of starting her search.

The LinkedIn model showcases connections based more on professional networking than the more social sites of Facebook and MySpace. It is also more detailed than the 140-character brief messages allowed to be posted on the Twitter site.

Searches on these sites for contacts or job opportunities should not be limited to just private enterprise. Government agencies are also discovering the advantages to having an online presence, and several have profiles on these sites. With more than 550,000 federal employees scheduled to retire during the next five years and the Obama administration looking to add another estimated 270,000 workers by 2012, many of these agencies will be frantic trying to find workers.

SOURCE: Lindberg, Joseph, and Ojeda-Zapata, Julio. "Facebook, Twitter, LinkedIn Can Lead to Jobs for Unemployed." *St. Paul Pioneer Press,* 18 October 2009.

11

Do's and Don'ts
Once You've Landed a Job

SURE, IT'S ENTICING TO CHECK your social media pages regularly while at work. But in today's environment, there are six people reportedly on the prowl for each and every job opening.[1] Clearly, this is not a good time to risk penalties for excessive and unwarranted use of Facebook, MySpace, Bebo, Twitter, or other social media on the job.

We've all heard of employees passed over for promotion, disciplined, or even pink-slipped for spending too much time using social media, posting a negative comment, revealing too much about themselves or their employer, or simply violating some aspect of their company's social media policy. So how do you avoid becoming someone else's object lesson?

"While you're at work," says Dave Kerpen, CEO of theKbuzz, a leading social media leveraging and word-of-mouth marketing firm, "Common sense is the best practice."

---

[1] Conaway, Laura. "Six Unemployed People for Every Opening." NPR.org, 9 October 2009 <http://www.npr.org/blogs/money/2009/10/six_unemployed_people_for_ever.html>.

Unfortunately, common sense is not necessarily all that common.

According to recent studies,[2] close to 17 percent of larger employers are unhappy with some of their employees' use of social media, up to and including the point of actually terminating at least one employee for social media misbehavior. That's double the number who got the boot for social media misuse in the previous year. Thousands of companies routinely investigate or discipline employees for violating social media policies or being too open with information online.

The Search Goes On

In all of this, employers are generally not looking for defamatory remarks, although they're likely to have those remarks and their sources pointed out by helpful social media users. They're more interested in reining in the loss of productivity that comes with unwanted social media activity. And those losses can be heavy. For example, a 2008 study of 776 British office workers by Global Secure Systems Ltd., a leading IT security company in the UK, identified some $9.5 billion per year in lost productivity due to employees who openly admitted wasting from 30 minutes to 3 hours per day with social media.[3]

Employers are even more concerned about the possibilities of identity theft and malware infestation that result from employees

---

[2] Ostrow, Adam. "Facebook Fired: 8% of US Companies Have Sacked Social Media Miscreants." *Mashable: The Social Media Guide,* 10 August 2009 <http://mashable.com/2009/08/10/social-media-misuse/>.

[3] Global Secure Systems. "Facebook Costs UK Billions." GSS Monthly Newsletter, 2008 February <http://www.gss.co.uk/newsletter/15/view/>.

visiting sites that really have no relationship to their work. Although some suggest this is paranoid, no one disputes that the heaviest usage of both pornographic and social media sites occurs during normal working hours.[4]

There was a time when you could easily hide your social media activities by switching to another application when your supervisor approached. But no longer. Modern IT departments can monitor every e-mail, text, online chat, and Internet site visit, flagging the worst offenders for more thorough investigations. This explains why many employees now interact with social media via smartphones, BlackBerrys, and the like.

Most IT departments report that in-house abuse of social media is worse than originally anticipated, driving nearly half of large employers to totally forbid social media access during the workday.[5] But even if your employer's IT team is deaf, dumb, and blind to your social media connectivity, you can still expect to get caught if you share too much about sensitive corporate matters or just make rude remarks about your employer.

What's an Employee to Do?

In face of this comprehensive on-the-job crackdown against wasting time and bandwidth on social media, employees who like their paychecks should follow a few basic best practices to keep from tweeting themselves out of a job. These include:

---

[4] Bisette, David C. "Internet Pornography Statistics 2003." HealthyMind.com, 2003 <http://www.healthymind.com/s-porn-stats.html>.

[5] Gaudin, Sharon. "Study: 54 Percent of Companies Ban Facebook, Twitter at Work." Wired.com, 9 October 2009 <http://www.wired.com/epicenter/2009/10/study-54-of-companies-ban-facebook-twitter-at-work>.

1. Keep working hard.

The most likely reason to lose your job due to your social media activities is the poor performance that results if you let your work and your play with social media get out of balance. To maintain a satisfactory balance, be sure to:

- Keep up your productivity.
- Maintain the quality of your deliverables.
- Meet all your deadlines.
- Preserve your work relationships in the offline world.

From a larger perspective, recognize that if your social media activities feel more compelling than your work, you're on a slippery slope and could easily slide right into the unemployment line. If you can switch to a job that's more interesting, your problems with social media temptations will be far less dangerous to your economic health. If you can't switch, see items two through six below.

2. Maintain time logs.

If your job includes legitimate usage of social media—for example, you're charged with monitoring and responding to social media mentions of your employer's products, services, and/or brand—keep an accurate log of where and when you're working on the social media. Make particular note of any valuable contacts you make, problems you identify, information you pick up, and discussions you join. Experts recognize that building a business depends not just on making connections via social networking but on monitoring and joining relevant social media discussions, then steadily establishing yourself (or your company) as a competent, reliable resource. With a detailed time log in hand, you'll have documentation that justifies your time and effort if any accusations come your way regarding your social media activities.

When your job does not include working the social media world, time logs are an even better idea. They'll enable you to keep track of how much paid time you're actually devoting to social media (much more accurate than your best guesstimates) and provide an early-warning mechanism to help you cut back before your employer catches on. Although it's true that taking a quick break in the world of social media can refresh you, getting lost there can ruin your viability on the job.

3. Set social media time limits, and stick to them.
More than half of large employers claim to forbid all access to social media sites during the day, so a large number of them—and almost certainly an even larger number of smaller companies—allow access. Employees who want to keep their jobs should therefore exercise self-restraint.

Once a month, go over your time logs, and identify those hours you spent with social media that you can justify and those you can't. This allows you to appropriately expand, to contract, or to maintain the number of hours you allocate to social media while you're working. Based on this documented pattern of social media activity, you can set your own realistic limits that will prevent a problem in the event that managerial attention turns your way.

4. Limit the personal and company information you disclose.
It is not just the fact of social media activity that lands employees in hot water. It's also the nature of those activities that actually triggers disciplinary actions, career limits, and termination. Yes, everyone has personality facets that can be let loose in appropriate surround-ings. The problem is that social media tends to tear down some of the barriers between surroundings, allowing your "Party Girl"

image to more easily leak back to your co-workers or your "Take This Job and Shove It" attitude to stand a better chance of crossing your supervisor's desk.

There are ways to reduce the chances of "blowback" from social media activities that you don't want known at work. But the best way to mitigate this danger is simply to withhold anything inappropriate in the first place. The general rule goes something like: "If you wouldn't want your mom, your favorite aunt, or your boss to see it, don't post it." For example:

- Limit your public postings about touchy subjects, such as politics or religion.
- Make sure your social media remarks reflect a law-abiding attitude.
- Keep those four-letter words and other epithets to a minimum.
- Beware of sexual innuendo or other R-rated content.
- Make no personal remarks about company management, co-workers, their families, friends and acquaintances, and anyone who might know them.

5. Turn off all social media notifications while at work.
Notifications of interesting posts, messages, news, and other information are among the nice things about social media. But not while you're on the clock for non–social media responsibilities. Get in the habit of turning off e-mails, tweets, RSS feeds, and other messaging systems first thing in the morning and leaving them off until you're safely away from your job.

If you're reluctant to turn them off, look into using the various software tools that let you divert these notifications and store them for later review.

6. Utilize opportunities to minimize social media time and exposure.
Automating links between more of your social media networks will
allow you to get more done with social media in far less time. For
example, tie your various networks together so posting a message
on Facebook automatically triggers the full range of tweets, blog
entries, and other postings you'd normally do by hand.

In addition, look into your social media networks' capabilities to
block unwanted contacts and to segment those contacts you retain.
This helps you limit your private information to the relatively
smaller circles of people you know and trust. Today's expanding
contact management and privacy capabilities offer many possibilities for keeping your work-related contacts more thoroughly
separate from your private life.

"In a lot of states," says Kerpen of theKbuzz, "you can't be fired
for things you do on your own time. Even so, everyone should be
conscientious about doing their job as well as they can and thinking
twice about the information they share. Above all, don't talk about
your company in a negative way online. That kind of thing has consequences."

12

Your Next Job Search Starts Now

ONCE A JOB SEEKER LANDS A JOB, the tendency is to close up shop on the job search. Particularly if securing the new job was an arduous process, the last thing a new hire wants to consider is additional strategizing when it comes to job search. Better to just hunker down and work the job you've just acquired.

Right? Wrong!

In fact, this strategy is what leaves so many job hunters feeling helpless and hopeless in the event of job loss. To come full circle with a topic we introduced earlier in this book, remember that the smarter approach is to view any new job as the first step in an ongoing cycle of search. By this we mean the search for promotion and advancement or for positioning in case of unexpected circumstances. In addition to planning a job-seeking strategy, job seekers must have a plan for after the job has been secured and how to parlay this into the next job. Such items as updating profiles, posting press releases, self-promoting a new position, internal and external communications using social networks, and remembering to thank all of those who helped you get the job (and return the favor by promoting others as applicable!) are the next steps in the process of career management.

Considerations in Career Management

There is a significant difference between a job search and career management. A job search is a single event most often started when one either loses a job or is seeking new employment. Once a satisfying new position is located, the search is over. Career management is much more of a mindset and is not a one-time event. Career management involves the setting of both long- and short-term goals, along with step-by-step goals for their obtainment. Career management does not end when a new job is located; rather the new job is viewed as one rung on the ladder to further professional growth and development. In this way, career management, unlike traditional job search, is an ongoing process that need never end.

Career Management Strategies

Career management involves several strategies that serve to distinguish this process from that of traditional job search. With career management, there is much more of a focus on the long-term rather than immediate-need gratification.

Developing a Career Vision

An important component of career management is to develop a vision for what constitutes "right livelihood." This vision should be broad enough to allow for flexibility, yet focused enough so that an action plan can be developed. It should be based on your most essential core values and incorporate all aspects of your personal brand. In this way, the vision will guide your choices in terms of an appropriate career path.

Commitment to Lifelong Learning

An important aspect of career management is a commitment to lifelong learning in order to sharpen both knowledge and skill set. This means keeping current with regard to labor market trends as well as new technology being implemented in the workplace. Continuing learning can take the form of reading, attending company-based seminars, or enrolling in coursework that can be either classroom-based or via distance-learning programs.

Resume Revision

Traditional job search usually entails the creation of one resume, which is then sent to numerous employers. The resume is then laid aside when new employment is obtained. Those with a focus on career management recognize the need to continually update their resumes as new skills and competencies are developed. It can also involve the creation of several versions of the resume to highlight the specific skill sets needed across different career paths. In either case, continual resume revision serves as notice to potential employers of your updated skills while also paving the way for you to pursue new opportunities as they arise.

Keeping Current in Job-Search Methods

Most people seeking a job are so busy reading job postings and submitting resumes that they do very little reading with regard to job-search trends. Those engaged in long-term career management do commit time to reading about new methods of job search, such as personal branding, Skype interviewing, or the use of social media. They are then in a great position to take advantage of this knowledge in designing an effective search strategy.

Building of Long-Term Relationships

Those involved with career management recognize that the development of long-term relationships is a continuing process involving those with whom we come in contact on a day-to-day basis. This can include co-workers, supervisors, colleagues, vendors, and clients. It can also extend to those relationships we develop as we pursue our interests and hobbies or attend spiritual and community events. It is well-acknowledged that over 70 percent of "hidden" job opportunities are discovered via networking efforts. With this in mind, be sure to hand your business card to everyone you meet, whether professionally or socially, and have your 15-second elevator pitch at the ready. This pitch is a capsule of your title and main job responsibilities.

You may also think about sending out a press release as an e-mail blast that describes your new job in terms of company information, your title, major responsibilities, and overall objectives over the coming year. Be sure to include your phone number and e-mail address.

You will also want to be sure and send thank-you letters to all those who assisted with your job search. Include a business card in all such correspondence, along with an offer to engage in cross-promotion of services through such options as guest blogging and referrals.

Career Management Using Web 2.0

In the world of Web 2.0, networking has expanded to include use of the social media sites to not only seek new employment but to promote your new job and to establish valuable contacts that can advance your career even further.

Update Your Profile

Update your social media profile with information regarding your current position and the company you work for. Include a listing of your major responsibilities and goals for the next six months to one year. Be sure to include any keywords so that your profile attracts colleagues and even future employers.

Learn from Others

A key benefit of starting a blog or having a Twitter account is that you have the opportunity to benefit from others' knowledge and experience via their feedback. This is a great way to begin developing rapport and to build important new connections.

Internal Communication

Just as you seek to promote yourself with external parties, you will also want to spread word of your new job within the company. Post comments to the company blog, or interact with clients/customers on the company social networking site. In this way, you will establish your reputation with key company stakeholders both within and outside the company.

Stay Current with Industry Trends

You might also want to consider opening a Google Reader Account and search those sites that are directly discussing your given industry. Your goal is to become well versed on every trend that is or will be affecting your industry. Post any relevant issues to your blog or Twitter feed, and encourage discussion. This will go a long way toward building your reputation as an expert.

Select the Best Sites

There are three basic criteria in choosing the best social media sites with which to promote yourself and your brand:

1. The volume of traffic that the site generates is important, because you want to promote yourself where there are many people in search of someone with your skills and knowledge. Such sites as LinkedIn, Facebook, or Twitter allow your brand to go viral through second- and third-level connections.
2. The credibility of the social networking sites helps ensure that your brand is targeted only to those successful individuals you wish to network with to advance your career.
3. The relevancy of the site to your career and industry is also a factor. There are sites created for specific professions, such as MedHunters for nurses and other health-care professionals and Blackboard for teachers.

Ning contains social networks for nearly every sector as well. You will want to become part of these specialized networks, because they offer targeted networking opportunities.

Social Media Marketing

Create a blog to which you post advice or news of relevance to your industry. In this way, readers will get to know your style and preferences. However, it is not enough to create a blog and hope it attracts attention. The reality is that it takes much more effort to market the blog than to actually write the content for it. There are several ways you can begin to market yourself using social media. These include joining groups and becoming an active member through asking questions or posting comments, guest posting on the sites of other blogs, and creating your own group or fan page. The goal is to become recognized as a thought leader in your particular industry by clients, colleagues, and potential new employers.

To be effective, you will need to be a consistent presence in whatever forums you join so that you gain name recognition. Make sure that whatever message you are putting out is aligned with the overall brand you wish to develop.

Establish a Professional Online Presence

Career management entails taking a very serious approach to establishing your online presence. You want to create content that will serve you well, regardless of whether it's read by a potential employer or client. Your posts should motivate readers to respond so that you may get a dialogue going. If you're using LinkedIn, don't be shy to ask for recommendations from past employers or clients who are also on the site. It's great to have 150 contacts but even better to have recommendations from at least some of them. These recommendations will help develop your professional reputation so that you may advance your career.

Conclusion

Throughout this book, we convey the ongoing theme that job seeking should not be seen as a periodic exercise but rather as an underlying mentality of ongoing professional development. When approached in this way, the pressure of finding yourself jobless will not be as great. Imagine having a resume, portfolio, network of contacts, and list of job possibilities at your disposal on any given day of the week. Your ability to focus on job satisfaction and professional advancement would be enhanced, and you would not have to worry about finding yourself in a position of joblessness without a starting point.

It's all about options. Even if someone is gainfully employed, an employee who perceives, rightly or wrongly, that changing jobs is not an option is at risk in a variety of ways. If you believe that you are stuck, you are much likely to suffer from burnout, depression, and sagging productivity. You always want to cultivate options for yourself. So always be on the lookout for that next job. You can always decline a job offer if you pursue a position but ultimately decide that it's not a step up from your current role.

We hope this book has been a step in that direction, and we wish you the best of luck with your job search and your ongoing professional advancement.

APPENDIX

Twitter Jobs and Job Sites

TWITTER JOBS
General Job Search:

@Accenture_jobs
@ADPcareers
@AlisonDoyle
@alistsolutions
@aoljobs
@Barry_at_IMPACT
@bostonrecruiter
@Brandyourself
@careerdiva
@CAREEREALISM
@CoolestJobs
@craigslistjobs
@DailyCareerTips
@danschawbel
@eexecutives
@ejobfairs
@elance_jobs
@employeefactor
@exectweets
@e4myJob
@fish4jobs
@Glassdoordotcom
@Indeed

@InterviewCoach
@jobangels
@JobConcierge
@jobhitsus
@jobhuntorg
@joblister
@jobseen
@jobsearch
@jobsforkarma
@Jobshouts
@jobs_now
@kellyjobs
@Keppie_Careers
@KijijiJobs
@linkedin_jobs
@LinkUp
@looktohire
@Microjobs
@MonsterCareers
@mycareers
@NowHiringJobs
@nytimescareers
@onlineresume
@OnlyUsJobs
@philreCareered
@PowerCV

@recruiterryan
@RecruitingTruth
@Simplyhired
@thejobsguy
@theonlinebeat
@twitjobsUSA
@USDOL
@workerswork
@WSJcareers
@YourJobStop

Geographic Region:

@AL_Jobs (Jobs in Alabama)

@apnijobs (Jobs in Pakistan, India, UAE, UK, and USA)

@aproductmanager (UK product managing/marketing jobs)

@AtlantaGAjobs (Jobs in Atlanta)

@atx_jobs (Jobs in Austin, TX)

@Canadajobbank (Jobs in Canada)

@careersindia (Jobs in India)

@caitjobs (California IT jobs)

@cdnjobforce (Canadian jobs)

@ColoradoSpgsJob (Jobs in Colorado)

@findajobindubai (Jobs in Dubai, UAE, and GCC countries)

@franceseojobs (SEO jobs in France)

@germanyseojobs (SEO jobs in Germany)

@home_jobs_india (Work from home jobs in India)

@IBMUKcareers (IBM careers in UK)

@IrishJobTweets (Jobs in Ireland)

@itjobssydney (IT jobs in Sydney)

@ITJobsTweet (IT and Internet jobs in UK)

@JobHits (UK job search)

@JobsAustralia (Jobs in Australia)

@JobsBoston (Jobs and advice in Boston area)

@jobschicago (Jobs in Chicago area)

@JobsCleveland (Jobs in Cleveland)

@jobsinsafrica (Jobs in South Africa)

@jobsinjobsbyref (Jobs in India)

@jobslosangeles (Jobs in Los Angeles area)

@jobsorlando (Jobs in Orlando area)

@jobsanfrancisco (Jobs San Francisco)

@jobssouthFL (Jobs in South Florida)

@journalism_jobs (Journalism jobs in UK)

@la_webjobs (Web jobs in Los Angeles)

@marketingjobny (Marketing jobs in New York)

@MNHeadhunter (IT jobs in Minnesota)

@mployd (Jobs in US, Canada, and the Philippines)

@mtltweetjobs (PR/Marketing/social media/tech jobs in Montreal)

@NewYorkTechJobs (Technology jobs in the greater New York area)

@nyprjobs (New York PR jobs)

@PRJobsLondon (London PR jobs)

@RichmondJobNet (Jobs in Richmond, Virginia)

@TopJobsInLondon (Jobs in London, UK)

@twitjobsuk (Jobs in UK)

Industry Type:

@ACTORSandCREW (Entertainment industry jobs and advice)
@alldevjobs (Developer jobs)
@AndreaSantiago (Health careers and advice)
@ArtDirectorJobs (Art director jobs)
@artinfojobs (Art industry jobs)
@authenticjobs (Tech and design jobs)
@coolclimatejobs (Climate and clean energy jobs)
@cwjobs (Copywriter jobs)
@DesignJobsLive (Design jobs)
@doscareers (Foreign Affairs)
@Ed2010News (Magazine advice)
@execSearches (Executive jobs)
@FitnessJobsUSA (Fitness jobs)
@GetAccountaJobs (Accounting jobs)
@GetChefJobs (Chef jobs)
@GetMarManagJobs (Marketing Manager jobs)
@GetPubRelatJobs (PR jobs)
@GreenEconomyNet (News and info on green jobs)
@greenerjobs (Green industry jobs)
@greenforall (Green-job industry info)
@GreenJobs (Green industry jobs)
@Jobs_Accounting (Accounting jobs)
@journalistics (Journalism advice)
@krop_jobs (Design and tech jobs)
@LibInfoSciJobs (Library and information science jobs)
@marketingpr (Marketing and PR jobs)
@mediabistro (News and info for media professionals)
@media_pros (Jobs for media professionals)
@narmsjobs (Retail and merchandising jobs)
@newretailjobs (Retail jobs)
@Pharmaceutical (Pharmaceutical jobs)
@photographyjobs (Photography)
@ppcjobs (SEM/PPC jobs)
@PRjobs (PR jobs and information)
@prsajobcenter (Public relations and corporate communication jobs)
@publishingjobs (Jobs in publishing industry)
@seojobs (SEO/SEM jobs)
@sfmobilejobs (Mobile Web and digital media jobs)
@smjobwire (Social media jobs)
@socialmediajob (Social media jobs)
@socialmediajobs (Social media jobs)

@TalentZooJobs (Ad, marketing, media, and digital jobs)
@usmusicjobs (Music industry jobs)
@Web_Design_Jobs (Web design and graphics jobs)

Company Name:

@1984jobs (Apple-related jobs)
@adidascareers (Jobs at Adidas)
@AllstateCareers (Jobs at Allstate)
@attjobs (Jobs at AT&T)
@Bkcareers (Jobs at Burger King)
@CBSI_Jobs (Jobs at CBS Interactive)
@comScoreCareers (Jobs at comScore)
@DaVitaJobs (Jobs at DaVita)
@DisneyABC (Jobs at Disney ABC media)
@easingaporejobs (Jobs at EA in Singapore)
@Ecolab_Jobs (Jobs at Ecolab)
@emccareers (Jobs at EMC)
@Ernst_and_Young (Ernst and Young careers)
@Expedia_Jobs (Expedia careers)
@forresterjobs (Jobs at Forrester Research)
@fullhousecareer (Jobs at Fullhouse Interactive)
@googlejobs (Jobs at Google)
@HewittCareers (Careers at Hewitt)
@Hyattcareers (Careers at Hyatt)
@JobsatIntel (Jobs at Intel)
@kissitocareers (Jobs at Kissito Post Acute)
@KrogerWorks (Jobs at Kroger)
@KWCareers (Keller Williams jobs)
@MattelRecruiter (Mattel jobs)
@mayoclinicjobs (Mayo Clinic jobs)
@MTVGamesJobs (MTV Networks games jobs)
@mtvnetworksjobs (Jobs at MTV)
@myspacejobs (Jobs at MySpace)
@NBCUniCareers (NBC Universal careers)
@oracle_jobs (Jobs at Oracle)
@pepsico_ukjobs (Jobs at Pepsi in UK)
@Raytheon_Jobs (Jobs at Raytheon)
@SonyJobs (Jobs at Sony)
@SiemensJobsUK (Jobs at Siemens in the UK)
@StarbucksJobs (Jobs at Starbucks)
@TRCareers (Jobs from Thomson Reuters)
@UPMCCareers (Careers at UPMC)

@UPSjobs (Jobs at UPS)

@VerizonCareers (Jobs at Verizon)

@washpostjobs (Jobs at the *Washington Post*)

@WBCareers (Jobs at Warner Brothers)

@WiproCareers (Jobs at Wipro)

@Work4AOL (Jobs at AOL)

Employment Type:

@AfterCollege (Networking for college students and graduates)

@allfreelance (Freelance jobs)

@buddingup (Students and new graduates)

@fashionintern (Fashion internships)

@findinternships (Internships)

@Freelancezone (Advice for freelancers)

@freelance_jobs (Freelance work)

@GetFreelanceJob (Freelance tech jobs)

@GradToGreat (Advice for graduate students)

@heatherhuhman (Advice for internship and entry-level job seekers)

@InternQueen (Internships)

@internweb (Internships)

@myfirstpaycheck (Jobs for teens)

@Project4Hire (Freelance and temporary jobs)

@StevenRothberg (Info for interns and recent grads)

@StudentJobs (Entry-level and student jobs)

@sweetcareers (Advice for college students and new grads)

@wahm_job_leads (At-home job leads)

@webfreelancejob (Freelance Web jobs)

@wFreelance (Freelance jobs)

@Work_Freelance (Freelance jobs)

@worldfreelance (Freelance jobs)

For Human Resource Professionals:

http://twitter.com/JobHuntOrg/recruiters-and-recruiting

http://twitter.com/kufarms/hr-social-media-recruitin

http://twitter.com/mflenory71/hr-and-od-professionals

http://twitter.com/philreCareered/recruiters

@hrcrossing (HR jobs)

@HRSearchPros (HR jobs)

@GetHRMgrJobs

Twitter Clients:

TweetMyJobs- http://www.tweetmyjobs.com/ (For job seekers and recruiters: Subscribe to desired job channels and get updates to your mobile phone)
TwitJobSearch- http://www.twitjobsearch.com/ (Search through global job opportunities posted to Twitter)
TwitHire- http://www.twithire.com/ (Compiles list of job postings to Twitter)
TwitterJobFinder- http://twitterjobfinder.com/ or http://twitterjobfinder.co.uk/ (Search engine using jobs posted to Twitter)
Mr. Tweet- http://mrtweet.com/ (Helps build a Twitter presence and identify relevant followers and news)
Twellow- http://www.twellow.com/ (Searchable directory of Twitter accounts)
Twibes- http://www.twibes.com/ (Join groups of Twitterers with common interests)
TweepML- http://tweepml.org/ (Manage and share groups of Twitter users)
Twitter Jobs- http://twitterjobs.org/ (Searchable database of job opportunities)
TweetAJob- http://tweetajob.com/ (Provides tools for recruiters and job seekers)
TweepSearch- http://tweepsearch.com/ (Search Twitter users' bios, friends, and followers)

Hashtags:

#career
#careers
#hiring
#joblisting
#jobposting
#job
#jobs
#jobsearch
#jobseeker
#jobtips
#recruiting
#resume

BONUS ONLINE EXTRAS:

Job Seekers' Readiness Checklist
Human Resources Checklist
Top 10 Tips for Job Seekers

Visit OnlineJobSearchBook.com

INTRODUCING...
The Social Media Survival Guide Series

Just as organizations and individuals are eager to embrace the opportunity, they are hesitant to take on additional risk, leaving many to fall behind the competition in the wake of uncertainty. **The Social Media Survival Guide** and its companion titles are designed to make social media accessible, tactical and easy to use right away. **The Survival Guide** series will help you to market successfully within this space, maintain a competitive edge and boost results—from increasing sales, to landing the job, to winning elections.

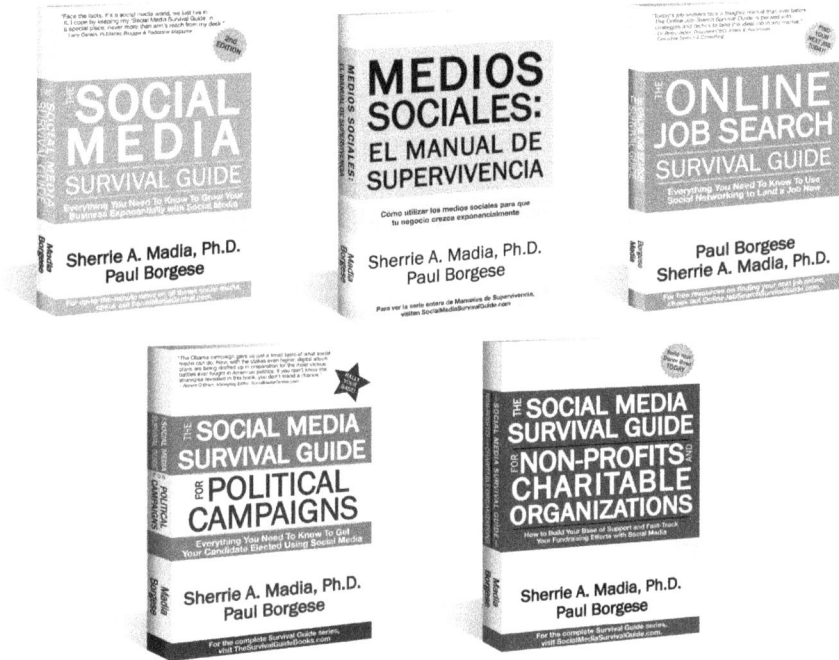

The Social Media Survival Guide:
Everything You Need to Know to Grow Your Business Exponentially with Social Media

The Social Media Survival Guide (Spanish-language edition)

The Online Job Search Survival Guide:
Everything You Need to Know to Use Social Networking to Land a Job Now

The Social Media Survival Guide for Political Campaigns:
Everything You Need to Know to Get Your Candidate Elected Using Social Media
(August 2010)

The Social Media Survival Guide for Nonprofit and Charitable Organizations: How to Build Your Base of Support and Fast-Track Your Fundraising Efforts with Social Media
(October 2010)

Order/Preorder at SocialMediaSurvivalGuide.com